おとなのORIGAMI-BOOK

cochaeの
グラフィック折り紙

Origami Lucky Charms

Bilingual, in Japanese and English

講談社

はじめに Introduction

　無病息災、開運招福、商売繁盛……昔から私たちの願望に終わりはありません。それらの願いを具現化し、人々に崇められてきたのが、異形の神々をはじめとする「縁起物」でした。「愛らしい神々を一堂に揃えたらどんなに楽しいだろう！」「どんなにおめでたいんだろう！」という純粋な興味がこの本を作るきっかけでした。

　私たちの「グラフィック折り紙」は、あらかじめ紙に図柄が描かれていることが特徴です。さまざまなテーマの作品を手がけていますが、いつも心がけているのは、私たちの折り紙を手に取った方々が、「折り紙」という伝統的な遊びに、これまでにない"可愛さ""面白さ"を感じることのできるものにする、ということです。今回の「めでた尽くし」でも、とにかく楽しくポップに、そして粋に折れることを考えて図柄を作りました。

　折り上げた作品は、四季折々の行事やおめでたい儀式にはもちろん、日常生活のなかでも気軽に飾ってみてください。いつでも側にいてくれる庶民的な神々が、きっとあなたを楽しく開運してくれるでしょう！

<small>こちゃえ</small>
cochae

目次 Contents

はじめに | 2
Introduction

めでた尽くし ラインナップ | 4
Origami Lucky Charms Lineup

縁起物好きの日本人 | 10
Talismans in Japan

cochaeの折り紙ワークショップ | 12
Cochae's Origami Workshop

基本の折り図記号 | 16
Basic Origami Folds

24枚のめでた尽くし 解説付き | 17
24 Origami Lucky Charms with Explanation

折り図 | 65
Instructions & Diagrams

この本の使い方
How to use this book.

● ミシン目で折り紙をカットし、
p65からの折り図を見ながら折ってみましょう。
Remove the paper designs by tearing along the perforated line, and fold using the instructions and diagrams from p65 onward.

● ☆マークは、難易度のレベルを表しています。
Stars express the degree of difficulty.

> ★　　簡単！ easy
> ★★　やや簡単 intermediate
> ★★★ ちょっと難しい more difficult

●「折り図記号」や、複数の折り方に共通する
「基本の折り方」は、p16を参照してください。
See p16, for an explanation of folding symbols and basic folds.

ししまい
獅子舞 ★
Shishimai

17

まねきねこ
招き猫 ★★
Maneki-Neko

19

つる
鶴 ★★
Crane

21

かめ
亀 ★
Turtle

23

姫だるま ★
ひめだるま
Hime-Daruma

25

うさぎ ★
Rabbit

27

海老 ★
えび
Lobster

29

おしどり「雌」★
Mandarin Duck

33

おしどり「雄」★
Mandarin Drake

31

ご祝儀袋 ★
_{ごしゅうぎぶくろ}
Goshūgi-bukuro

35

かえる ★
Frog

37

お狐さま ★★
_{おきつねさま}
Okitsune-sama

39

扇子 ★
_{せんす}
Sensu

41

恵比寿 ★★★
Ebisu
43

大黒天 ★★
Daikokuten
45

福禄寿 ★★
Fukurokuju
47

布袋、毘沙門天、寿老人、弁財天 ★
Hotei, Bishamonten, Jurōjin, Benzaiten
49

ふじさん
富士山 ★
Mount Fuji

51

こけし ★
Kokeshi Doll

53

かぶと
兜 ★
Warrior's Helmet

55

たい
鯛 ★
Sea Bream

57

おかめ ★
Okame

―

59

さるぼぼ ★★
Sarubobo

―

61

ふくすけ
福助 ★
Fukusuke

―

63

縁起物好きの日本人

　日本人はとかく、めでたいものが好きな国民です。古来の伝統や風俗が失われつつあるといわれる現在でも、身の回りを見渡してみれば、昔ながらの「縁起物」の数々が、ひそかに存在を主張しているはずです。

　そんな「縁起物」が、俄然、活気づくのがお正月です。初日の出を仰ぎ、初詣で破魔矢をもらい、正月2日には「一富士二鷹三茄子（なすび）」の初夢を願い眠りにつく。さらに、門松や注連縄（しめなわ）で玄関先を飾り、床の間には鏡餅、柳箸でお節料理やお雑煮を頂く──日本人の一年は、おめでたい「縁起物」尽くしで幕を開けるのです。

　そもそも「縁起物」の由来は、神社やお寺などの由緒書きを描いた「縁起」にあります。遠くまで参拝にいけない人々のために配った「縁起（由緒書き）」に代わって、破魔矢や絵馬、鈴、人形など、各々の寺社のご利益にあやかれそうな品物が登場し、これが「縁起物」として人々の暮らしに浸透していきました。

　数多の縁起物が生まれ、今なお親しまれている背景には、人々の普遍的な願いがあります。その願いとは「開運招福」、つまり「現世利益」です。商売繁盛から、無病息災、家内安全、不老長寿、開運招福など、そのご利益は枚挙にいとまがありません。一神教の国々とは異なり、日本の"八百万（やおよろず）の神"にはご利益分担があり、人々はそれぞれの願いに応じた神さまを信じ、縁起物を求めてきたのです。

　本書で紹介するのは、日本人なら誰もが知っている「めでたいもの」ばかり。「七福神」や「福助」といった"ラッキー・ゴッド"をはじめ、「富士山」「鶴」「亀」「さるぼぼ」など、長い歴史のなかで縁起のよいものとして愛され続けてきたものです。日頃、忙しくて福を願う気持ちもどこかに消し飛んでしまっている方も、この本で「めでたいもの」を折ってみてください。きっと福々とした気持ちになれることでしょう。

＊本書では、明治から昭和にかけて流行した引札（ひきふだ）（商店などが配布したチラシ）を中心に縁起物が描かれた絵図を収録しています。折り紙とあわせてお楽しみ下さい。

Talismans in Japan

Japanese people tend to be fond of anything auspicious. Even now, when ancient traditions and customs are said to be disappearing, a glance around will surely reveal many traditional talismans quietly persisting in all kinds of places.

These lucky charms suddenly come into their own at New Year's. People climb mountains to greet the first sunrise of the year at the summit, receive a sacred arrow called a *hamaya* upon making their first shrine visit of the year, and go to sleep hoping to dream of the three auspicious objects, Mount Fuji, a hawk, and an eggplant. They also adorn the entrance to their home with a *kadomatsu* decoration made from pine and bamboo and a straw *shimenawa* festoon, place a *kagami-mochi* mirror-shaped rice cake in their *tokonoma* alcove, and use willow chopsticks to eat special New Year's food like *osechi* delicacies and *ozōni* soup. Japanese people see in the New Year with all kinds of lucky charms!

The Japanese word for lucky charms is *engimono*, which derives from *engi*, or the narratives about the historical origins of a shrine or temple. It came to refer to a written record of these stories delivered to worshippers unable to travel long distances, and eventually to objects related to the good fortunes of a shrine or temple, such as the *hamaya* arrow, *ema* votive tablets, bells, figurines, and so forth. These objects have come to be a part of people's everyday lives. There are many *engimono*, and even now these familiar forms represent a universal wish. That wish is for good luck—or in other words, divine favor. From a profitable business to good health, a happy family, longevity, good luck—the list of divine favors is endless. Unlike countries with a monotheistic religion, Japan's myriad deities are required to bestow their favors. People believe in the gods that grant their various wishes, and for this they need lucky charms.

The auspicious objects presented in this book will be familiar to any Japanese. The so-called "lucky gods" such as the Shichifukujin or Seven Gods of Good Fortune, and Fukusuke the god of commerce, as well as objects like Mount Fuji, cranes, turtles, and *sarubobo* figurines have all been treasured talismans for centuries. Even if you are too busy to rely on luck, please try your hand at making the objects in this book. We guarantee you'll soon be feeling as lucky as can be!

「めでた尽くし」折り紙をもっとめでたく！
cochaeの折り紙ワークショップ
Cochae's Origami Workshop

招福「飾り熊手」をハンドメイド
A handmade lucky decorative rake

あらゆる福を搔き集めるという「飾り熊手」。ホームセンターなどで売っている熊手に「めでた尽くし」の折り紙を飾り付ければ、ポップな縁起物のできあがり。

This is a lucky charm for raking in good fortune. You can make a plain bamboo rake available in most home centers into an auspicious object by decorating it with origami lucky charms.

材料
- 「めでた尽くし」折り紙————お好みの作品を
- 熊手————1本
- 折り紙(赤:12×15cm)————4枚
- 稲穂————数本
- 招福グッズ————お好みで

What you need
- Your favorite origami lucky charms
- Bamboo rake
- Red folding paper(12×15cm)———— 4 sheets
- Several ears of rice
- Other favorite auspicious objects

"招福グッズ"として欠かせない小判、水引、鈴、「大入」の札などを用意。
Typical auspicious objects include the oblong gold coins called *koban*, red-and-white cords, little bells, and tags printed with the characters 大入 to bring in good luck.

御幣の作り方　How to make a *Gohei* strip

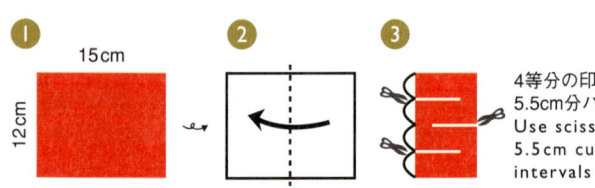

① 15cm / 12cm / 裏返す Turn over.
②
③ 4等分の印をつけ、交互に5.5cm分ハサミを入れる / Use scissors to make 5.5cm cuts at equal intervals as shown.

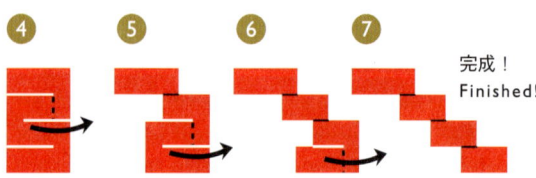

④ ⑤ ⑥ ⑦ 完成！Finished!

稲穂と鈴はワイヤーで留め、小判は瞬間接着剤で貼ります。
Use wire to attach the ears of rice and bells, and stick the *koban* on with superglue.

一.
好みの招福グッズを付ける
Decorate the rake with auspicious objects.

二.
折り紙で御幣を作って飾る
Attach origami *gohei* strips.

赤の折り紙で作った紅白の御幣と「大入」の札、水引を貼ります。
Complete with the red-and-white *gohei* strips and the 大入 printed tag.

三.
「めでた尽くし」折り紙のなかから好みの作品を飾って、できあがり
Attach your favorite origami lucky charms to finish off.

cochaeの折り紙ワークショップ
Cochae's Origami Workshop

「七福神」の乗り物「宝船」を作る
The "Treasure Ship" to carry the Seven Gods of Good Fortune

幸せを呼ぶ「七福神」はいつも宝船に乗っています。お好みの紙で宝船を折って、折りあげた「七福神」を乗せてみましょう。ユーモラスで縁起のいい飾り物が出来上がります。正月飾りにも最適！

Beloved by all for bringing us happiness, the Seven Gods of Good Fortune always travel in a boat known as the Treasure Ship. Make the Treasure Ship and place the origami figures of the gods in it for a humorous and auspicious ornament. Perfect for New Year's too!

材料
● お好みの紙（40×40cm）

What you need
● Paper（40×40cm）

宝船の折り方　How to make the Treasure Ship

❶  40cm / 40cm

❷ 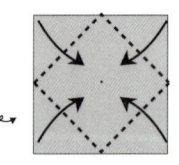 裏返す / Turn over.

❸ 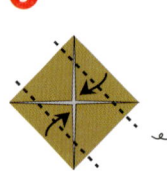 向きを変える / Turn round.

❹ 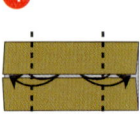 折り線を付ける / Make creases.

❺ 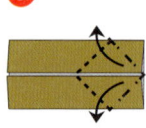 折り線を使って開きながらつぶす / Open out and flatten along the creases.

❻ 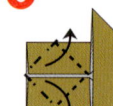 5と同様に、開きながらつぶす / Do the same on the other end.

❼  後ろへ山折り / Fold back using a mountain fold.

⑧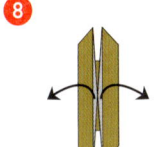
矢印の方へ開く
Open out in the direction of the arrows.

⑨
矢印の方へ開いてつぶす
Open out in the direction of the arrows and flatten.

⑩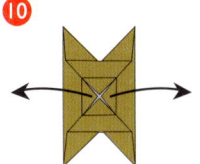
引き出す
Pull out.

⑪

⑫
裏返す
Turn over.

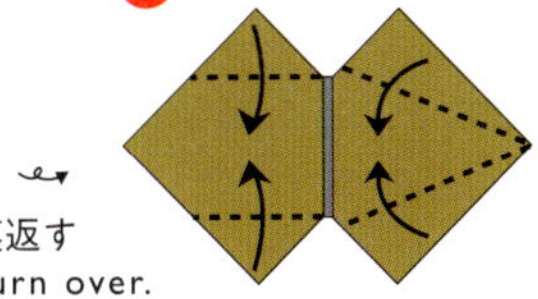

⑬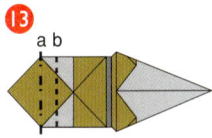
a b

aを山折りしてから、
2枚まとめてbを谷折り
Make a mountain fold at ⟨a⟩, and then with both sheets together make a valley fold at ⟨b⟩.

⑭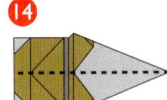
半分に谷折り
Fold in half using a valley fold.

⑮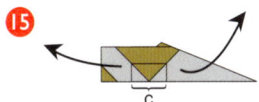
c

cが船底になるよう矢印の方へ引き上げ、
形を整える
Pull in the direction of the arrows to open it out.

完成！
Finished!

基本的な折り図記号を覚えよう
Basic Origami Folds

折り紙を折る前に、折り図の記号を覚えましょう。
これさえ覚えれば、折り図（p65〜）が簡単にわかります。

Before starting on your origami, familiarizing yourself with these basic folds will make it easier to follow the instructions (which begin on page 65).

移動線 Direction line

紙の移動を表します。矢印の始点と終点をよく見て、どのように移動しているかを確認しましょう。

Look carefully at the starting and end points of the arrow: it will show you the direction the paper needs to be folded.

谷折り Valley fold

 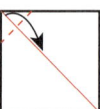 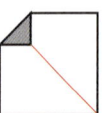

山折り Mountain fold

 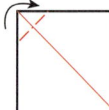 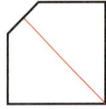

折り線をつける Make a crease

 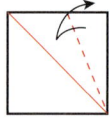

1つの図で表しますが、実際には2工程あります。
There is just one crease in the diagram shown here, but sometimes there are as many as three.

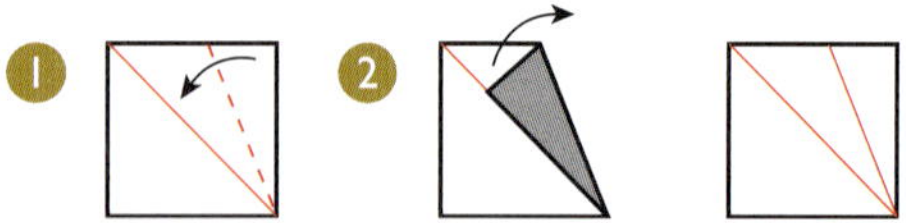

中割り折り Inside reverse fold

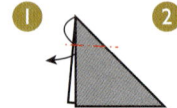 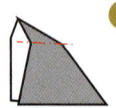 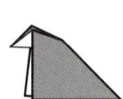

鶴の頭の折り方も、中割り折りですね。
An inside reverse fold is used on the crane's head, too.

かぶせ折り Outside reverse fold

段折り Stair fold

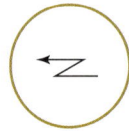 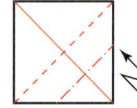 

16

獅子舞
Shishimai

正月の風物詩。日本最古の芸能のひとつで、厄除けや五穀豊穣など、さまざまな祈願を込めて舞われます。獅子頭をかぶれば頭痛に効き、獅子に噛んでもらうと賢くなるといわれます。正月の飾りものにぴったり。

The Lion Dance is a feature of New Year's. It is one of the oldest entertainments in Japan. Wearing the lion mask is said to cure headaches, and if you can get the lion to bite you, you'll apparently get smarter.

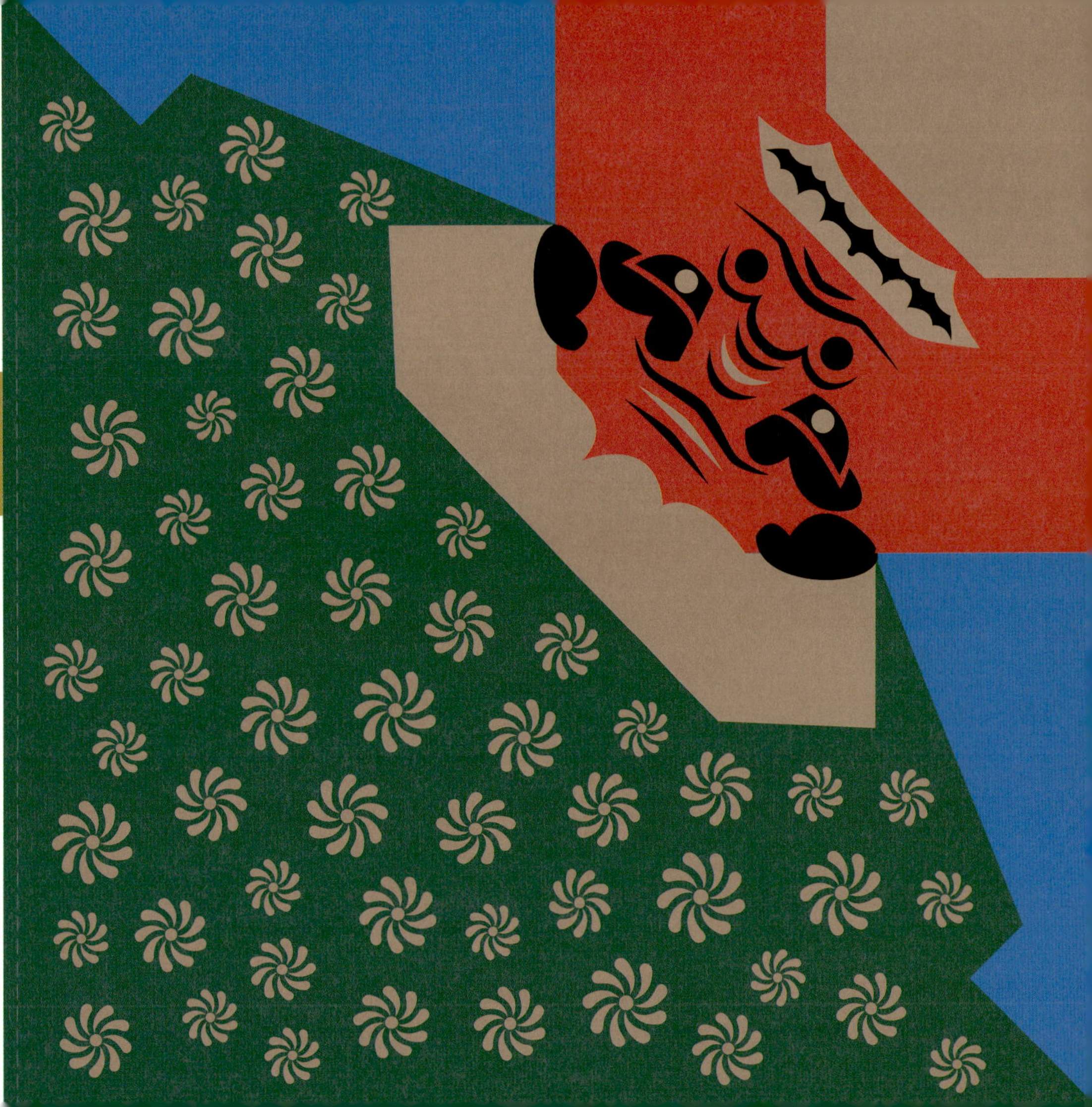

→ 折り図 p65

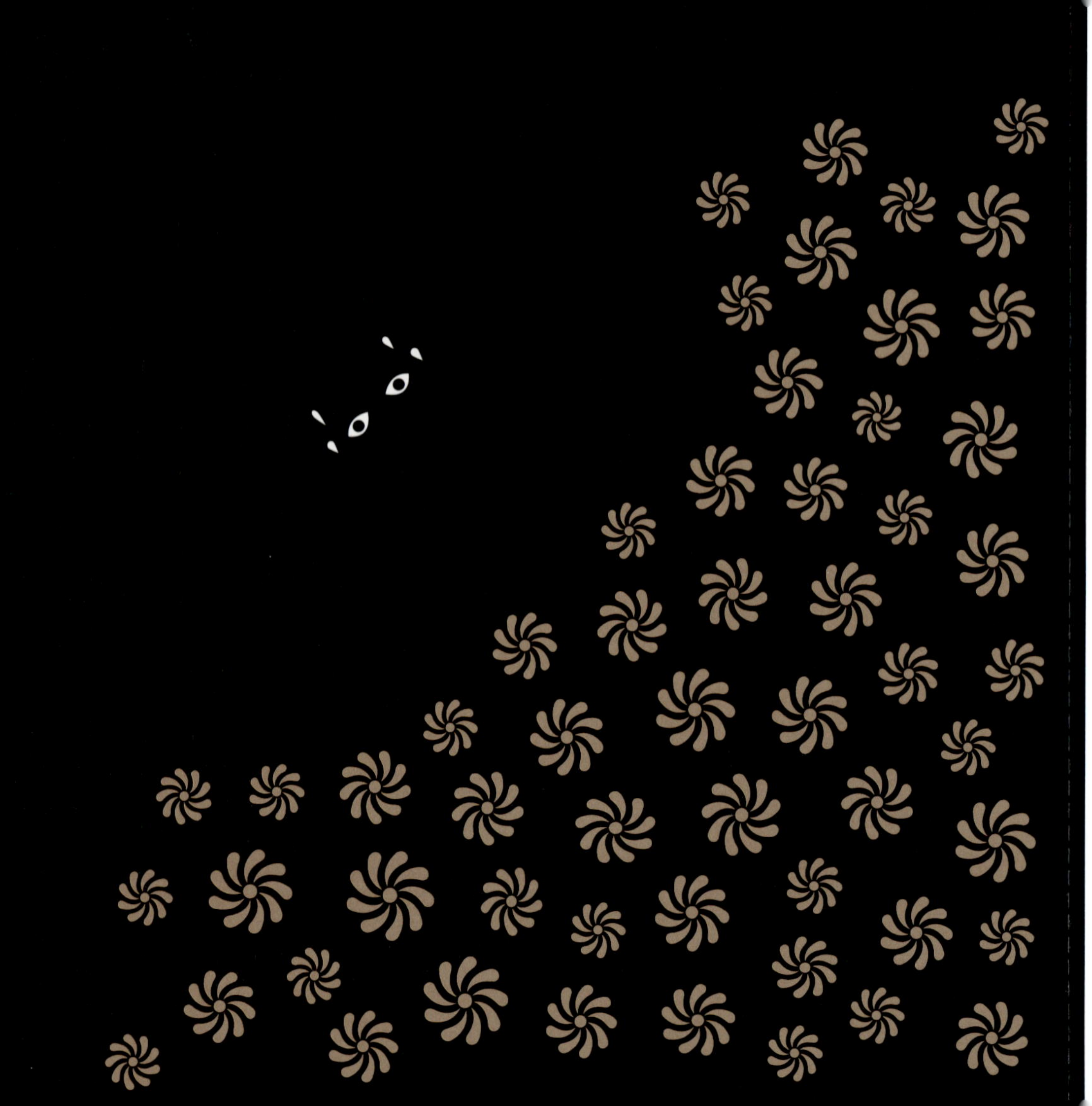

獅子舞
ししまい
Shishimai

アド・ミュージアム 東京

引札「金田屋商店　美人の獅子舞の図」(部分)。

招き猫
まねきねこ
Maneki-Neko ★★

左手を挙げると〈お客〉、右手なら〈お金〉を招きます。挙げた手の高さが高いほど、遠くの福を招きます。金運アップのラッキー・アイテムとして身近に飾ってみては。

A cat figure beckoning with its left paw will attract customers, and with its right, money. The higher its paw is raised, the further afield it will attract luck. Keep this lucky item by your side to bring luck with money.

→ 折り図 p66

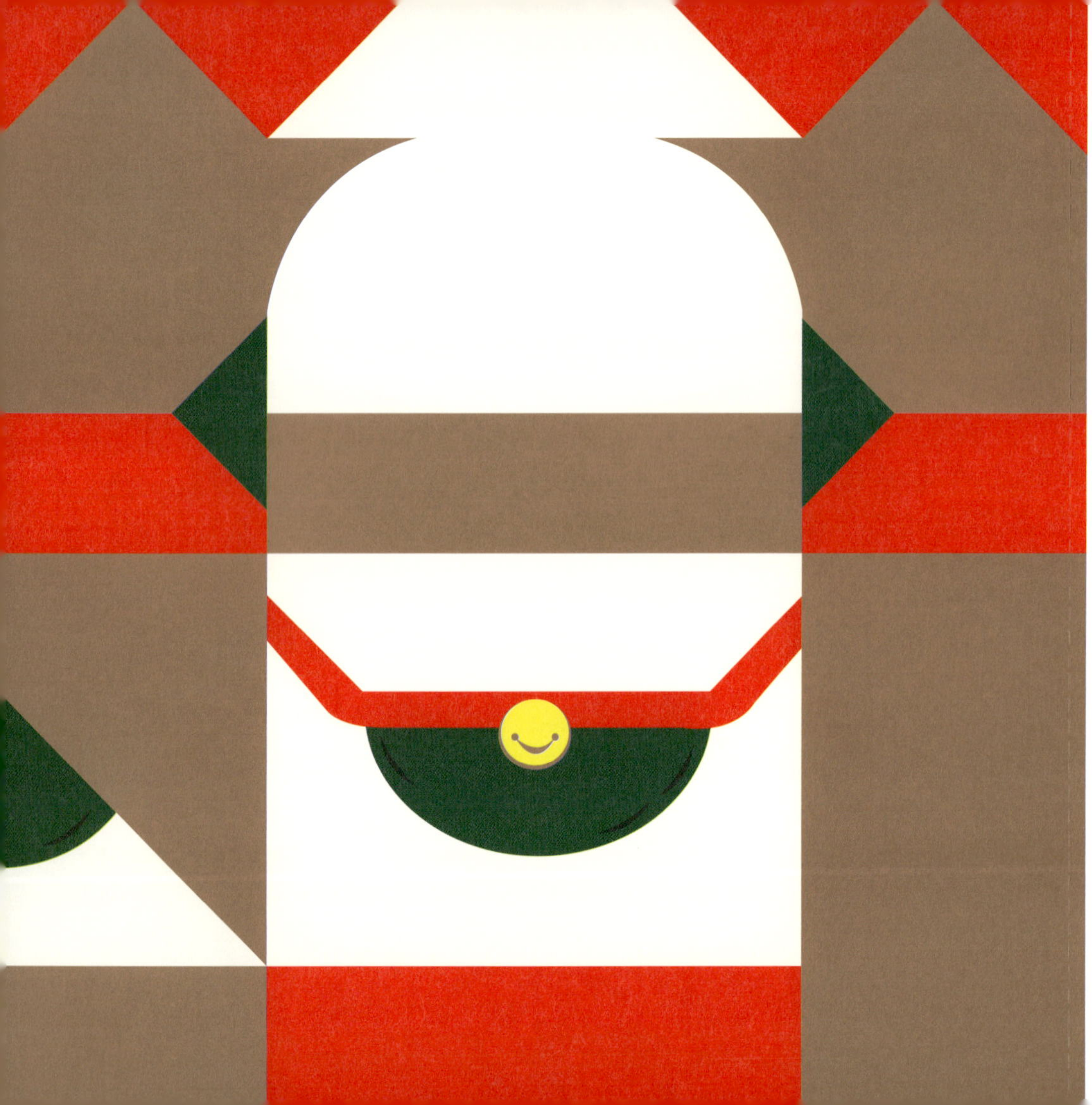

まねきねこ
招き猫
Maneki-Neko

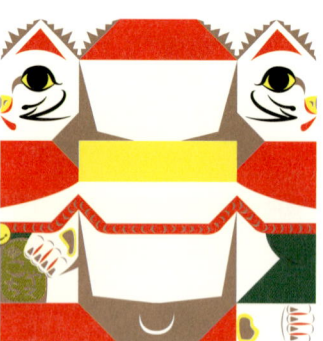

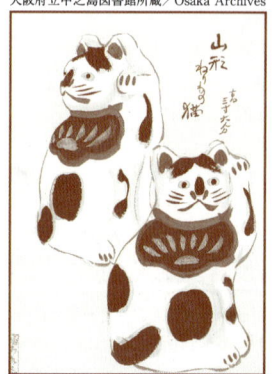

大阪府立中之島図書館所蔵／Osaka Archives

大正から昭和の郷土玩具や縁起物を集めた『巨泉玩具帖』(川崎巨泉)に描かれた猫の郷土玩具(部分)。

鶴(つる)
Crane

★★

「鶴は千年、亀は万年」という諺もあるように、古くから齢(よわい)の長い仙禽(せんきん)とされてきました。亀と一緒に、お正月やお祝い事の食卓に飾れば、めでたいムードを演出できます。

A proverb states, "The crane lives a thousand years, the turtle ten thousand years." Since ancient times the crane has been believed to be the long-lived bird from the pure realm of the immortals. Together with the turtle, it is used to decorate the dinner table at New Year's and other celebrations to create an auspicious mood.

→ 折り図 p68

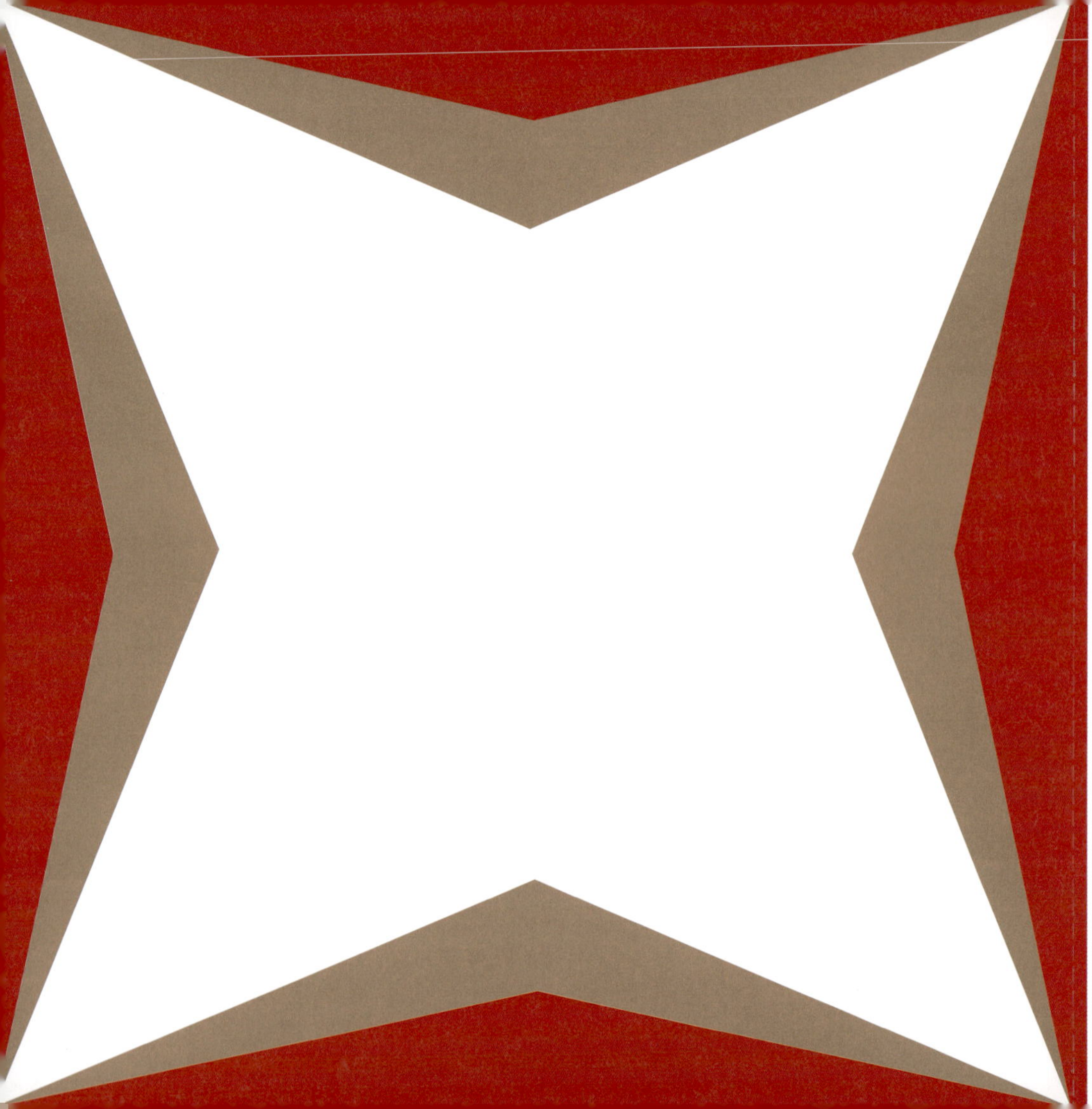

つる
鶴
Crane

アド・ミュージアム 東京

引札「新潟なかや旅館　松之山温泉場　三羽の鶴と松」(部分)。

亀 (かめ)
Turtle

長寿の縁起物。とくに、甲羅にふわふわと藻を生やした亀は、「蓑亀(みのがめ)」と呼ばれ、珍重されてきました。神亀(じんき)(724〜729年)や宝亀(ほうき)(770〜781年)など、珍しい亀の発見を機に改元された例もあります。

The turtle is also a talisman for longevity. The discovery of a new turtle has even been known to occasion a change in the name of the era, such as Jinki (literally "divine turtle," 724–729) and Hōki ("treasure turtle," 770–781).

亀
Turtle

引札「亀岡酒店　亀に乗る恵比寿」(部分)。

姫だるま
ひめだるま
Hime-Daruma

子どもの健やかな成長を願って贈られる姫だるま。愛媛県や大分県で作られ、みやげ物として人気です。女児誕生のお祝いのカードなどに添えるとかわいいでしょう。

The Hime-Daruma, or Princess Daruma doll, is a charm for the healthy growth of a child. They are also popular souvenirs from Ehime and Ōita prefectures in western Japan, where they are made, and make a really cute gift on occasions like the birth of a daughter.

→ 折り図 p71

姫だるま
ひめだるま
Hime-Daruma

全国の郷土玩具を集めた『玩具図譜』(尾崎清次)に描かれた姫だるま。

うさぎ
Rabbit

古くから、子孫繁栄のご利益があると信じられてきたうさぎ。勢いよく跳ねる姿から、「飛躍」をもたらす縁起物ともされています。入学のお祝いなどに添えてみてはいかがでしょう。

Since olden times the rabbit has been believed to bestow the gift of children. Because it hops around so energetically, it is also a talisman for great achievements. How about giving one to someone just starting college?

→ 折り図 p72

うさぎ
Rabbit

うさぎをモチーフにした引札見本。卯年の年始の挨拶に、商店などが配布した。

海老 (えび)
Lobster

姿かたちが、腰の曲がった老人を連想させることから、長寿の象徴とされ、「海の翁(おきな)」などといわれます。ゆでると赤くなるところも、めでたさ度アップの要因。一枚から、赤と青の2匹が折れます。

The lobster's shape resembles an old man bent over at the hip, for which it has become a symbol of longevity dubbed "Old Man of the Sea." Also, when boiled it turns red, which is an auspicious color. From a single sheet of paper you can make two lobsters, one red and one blue.

→ 折り図 p73

海老
えび
Lobster

アド・ミュージアム 東京

引札「信州諏訪上原長十郎商店
恵比寿、大黒、海老」(部分)。

おしどり「雄」
Mandarin Drake

「おしどり夫婦」「鴛鴦の契り」といわれるように、おしどりといえば、昔から仲の良い夫婦の象徴。夫婦円満の縁起物として、結婚祝いや結婚記念日などの贈り物に添えるとよいでしょう。

Mandarin ducks and drakes have long been a symbol for a loving couple, as reflected in several popular sayings. As a talisman for matrimonial happiness, they make a great present for a marriage ceremony or wedding anniversary.

→ 折り図 p74

おしどり「雄」
Mandarin Drake

歌川広重『花鳥錦絵』から「鴛鴦」（部分）。

おしどり「雌」
Mandarin Duck

夫婦円満の象徴とされるおしどりですが、実際には、毎年パートナーを替えています。子育ても、雌だけのお仕事です。

Mandarin ducks and drakes may be a symbol for wedded bliss, but in actual fact they swap partners each year. Rearing the ducklings is strictly the female's work.

→ 折り図 p75

おしどり「雌」
Mandarin Duck

歌川広重『花鳥錦絵』から「雪笹に鴛鴦」（部分）。

ごしゅうぎぶくろ

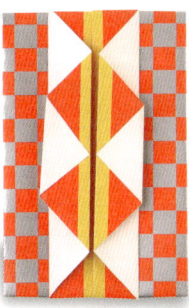

ご祝儀袋 ★

Goshūgi-bukuro

心付けを、紙に包んで渡すのは、日本人ならではの心遣いでしょう。ご祝儀袋やポチ袋には、縁起のよい意匠の文様や水引がつきものです。

Japanese people's solicitude for others is reflected in the practice of giving money in an envelope. Decorative envelopes for this purpose are embellished with a lucky design, with red-and-white cords.

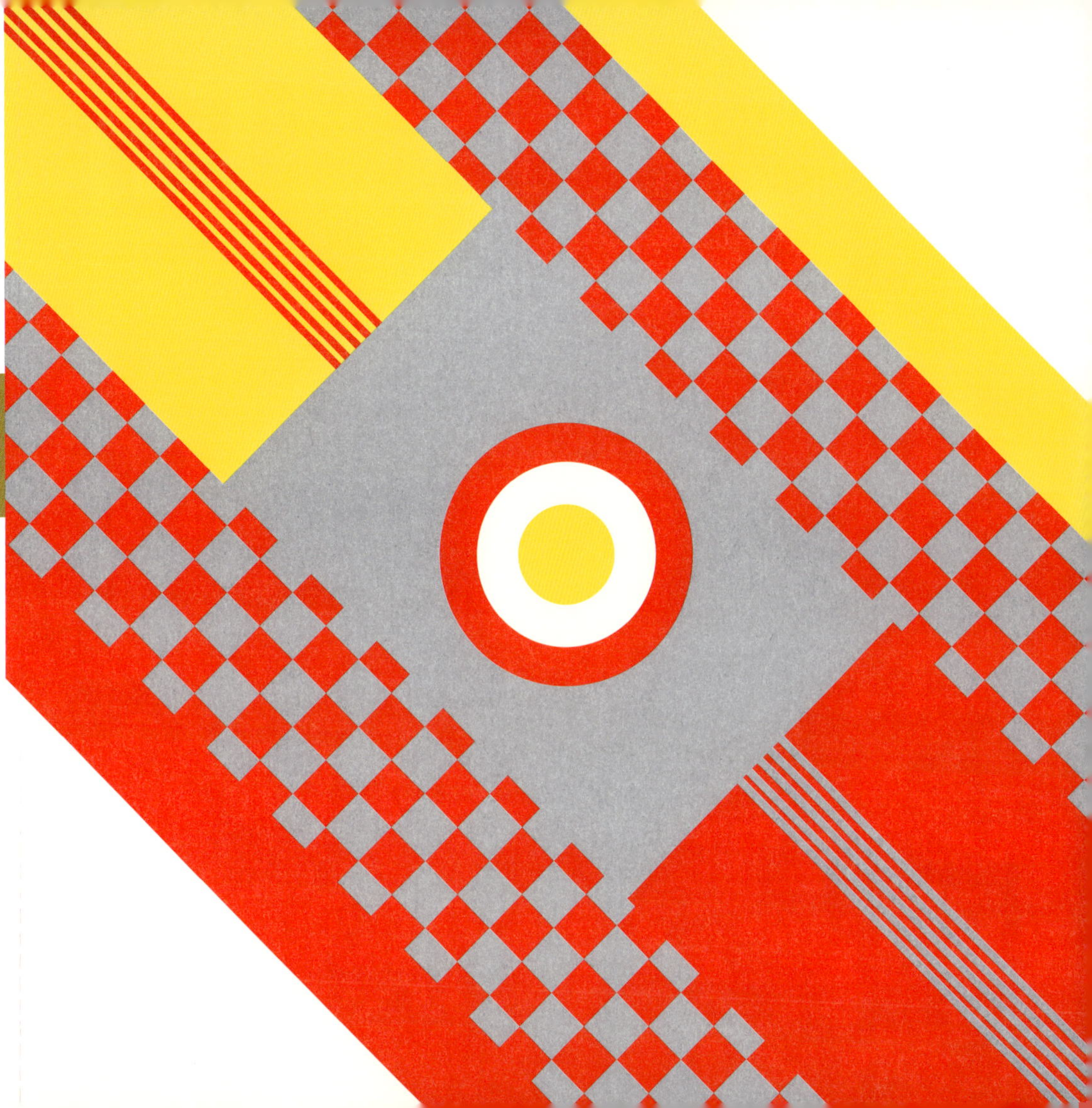

→ 折り図 p76

ご祝儀袋
Goshūgi-bukuro

かえる
Frog

田んぼの害虫を食べてくれるうえに、雨降りを予知するかえるは、日本では田の神の使いと考えられてきました。また、「無事かえる」「若がえる」「銭かえる」などの語呂合わせから、縁起物としても人気です。

As well as eating insects, frogs also predict rainfall, so in Japan they are believed to be the messenger of the god of rice fields. Furthermore, in Japanese they are called *kaeru*, which rhymes with expressions meaning "come home safely," or "become young again," making them popular lucky charms.

→ 折り図 p77

かえる
Frog

お狐さま
おきつねさま
Okitsune-sama ★★

日本全国津々浦々にまで浸透している田の神「お稲荷さん」。その仮の姿、あるいは使いとして信仰されているのがお狐さまです。

The god of rice fields throughout Japan is Oinari-san, and the fox deity Okitsune-sama is believed to be either the earthly incarnation or messenger.

→ 折り図 p78

お狐さま
Okitsune-sama

大阪府立中之島図書館所蔵／Osaka Archives

『巨泉玩具帖』に描かれた「伏見の狐」の置き物（部分）。

せんす
扇子
Sensu

開くと先が広がっていることから「末広」と呼ばれる扇。古来、末広がりの福を願う縁起物とされてきました。慶事の贈答品などに添え物として用いてもよいでしょう。表と裏で異なる仕上りを楽しんでください。

A folding fan, or *sensu* is a lucky charm for ever-increasing prosperity, and is often given alongside a gift on a congratulatory occasion. You can choose which side of the paper you like best for its upper side.

→ 折り図 p86

せんす
扇子
Sensu

アド・ミュージアム 東京

引札「染木綿手拭商大阪森田留二朗　鶴、扇子、翁の面」(部分)。

42

恵比寿
えびす
Ebisu
★★★

七福神のなかで唯一の日本生まれ。商売繁盛の神様として、絶大な人気を誇ります。恵比寿は「三郎」という名で大黒の弟だという説もあるので、大黒とセットで「恵比寿大黒」として飾ってもいいでしょう。

Ebisu is the only one of the Seven Gods of Good Fortune born in Japan. As the god of commerce, he is enormously popular. There is also a theory that Ebisu is actually younger brother of the god of wealth, Daikoku, so the two are often paired in ornaments and artwork.

→ 折り図 p80

恵比寿
えびす

Ebisu

アド・ミュージアム 東京

引札「富山広貫堂　恵比寿」(部分)。七福神は、引札の図柄としてとりわけ好まれた。

44

大黒天
だいこくてん
Daikokuten ★★

七福神は、もともと恵比寿と大黒の二神から始まりました。そのせいか、大黒さまはインド生まれながら、今でも福徳の神として、恵比寿と人気を二分しています。

The Seven Gods of Good Fortune were originally just two: Ebisu and Daikoku. Maybe that's why even though Daikoku was originally from India, as the god of wealth he is still as popular as Ebisu.

→ 折り図 p82

だいこくてん
大黒天
Daikokuten

アド・ミュージアム 東京

引札見本「大黒に日の丸」(部分)。

福禄寿
ふくろくじゅ
Fukurokuju ★★

身長わずか3尺（約90cm）、頭が長く髭の多い福禄寿。齢数千年と七福神きっての長生きで、幸福・高禄・長寿の三つを兼ね備えた福の神です。

Fukurokuju is about 90cm tall, with an elongated head and bushy beard. At several thousand years of age he is the oldest of the Seven Gods of Good Fortune, and bestows happiness, wealth, and longevity.

47　→ 折り図 p84

福禄寿
Fukurokuju

引札見本「福禄寿に鶴」(部分)。

48

布袋、毘沙門天、寿老人、弁財天
Hotei, Bishamonten, Jurōjin, Benzaiten

太鼓腹の布袋（招福の神）、勇ましい毘沙門天（戦いの神）、徳の高そうな寿老人（長寿の神）、紅一点の弁財天（芸能の神）。他の三神と合わせて「七福神」の出来上がりです。

The potbellied Hotei is the god of good luck, the brave Bishamonten is the god of warriors, the virtuous Jurōjin is the god of longevity, and the lone female of the group, Benzaiten, is goddess of the arts. Added to the previous three, these four complete the Seven Gods of Good Fortune.

→ 折り図 p87

布袋、毘沙門天、寿老人、弁財天
Hotei, Bishamonten, Jurōjin, Benzaiten

アド・ミュージアム 東京

引札「七福神　満徳・貞房画」。

富士山
ふじさん
Mount Fuji

めでたい図像の代表格、富士山。初夢といえば「一富士二鷹三茄子」です。一枚で、赤、青、緑、茶、4色の富士山を楽しむことができます。

Mount Fuji is the best-known symbol of good luck. It is the first on the list of lucky dreams at New Year's, followed by a hawk and eggplant. With just one sheet of paper you can enjoy Mount Fuji in red, blue, green, and brown.

51　→ 折り図 p88

富士山
ふじさん
Mount Fuji

歌川豊国「名勝八景　富士暮雪」
(部分)。

こけし
Kokeshi Doll

東北各地の温泉地で作られ、みやげ物として人気の伝統こけし。厄除け玩具の「除子」に由来するといわれます。女の子の初節句のお祝いなどに添えるとかわいいでしょう。

Kokeshi dolls are traditionally made in the hot spring areas of northern Japan, and are popular souvenirs. They are said to originate in the *yokeshi* toys made to ward off evil, and make a cute gift for a girl on the occasion of her first Girls' Festival.

→ 折り図 p89

こけし
Kokeshi Doll

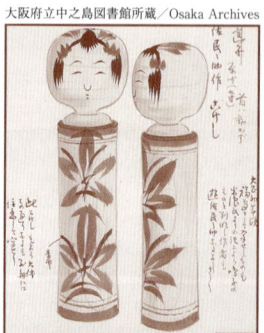

『巨泉玩具帖』に描かれた鳴子のこけし(部分)。

54

かぶと
兜
Warrior's Helmet

5月5日の端午の節句につきもののかぶと。日本では古来、男の子の初節句には、健やかな成長を祈願して、かぶとを贈る習慣があります。赤と青、好みで折ってください。

This decoration is popular for the Boys' Festival on May 5th. It is the customary in Japan to give a boy a helmet on the occasion of his first Boys' Festival. You can make it red or blue as you wish.

→ 折り図 p90

兜
かぶと

Warrior's Helmet

諷刺画「子供遊端午のにぎわい」
に描かれた兜人形（部分）。

56

鯛
たい
Sea Bream

日本人はとにかく、鯛が大好き。姿がよく美味、色は"祝儀の色"赤で、「めでたい」の語呂合わせまでついてくる——おめでたい席には欠かせない魚とされる所以です。

Japanese people just love sea bream whatever the occasion. It not only looks delicious, but it is red, the lucky color, and its Japanese name *tai* rhymes with the word *medetai*, meaning "auspicious." It certainly doesn't lack for lucky symbols!

→ 折り図 p91

鯛
Sea Bream

アド・ミュージアム 東京

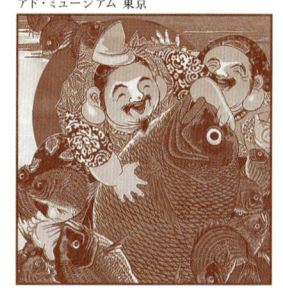

引札「魚問屋川上伊作　恵比寿、大黒、鯛」(部分)。

58

おかめ
Okame

円顔ででこっぱち、鼻は低くて下膨れのおかめさん。その福々しい面立ちから福を招くとされ、「お多福」とも呼ばれます。商売の神、福助のお嫁さんという説もあるので、夫婦円満の願いを込めて、並べて飾ってみては。

Okame's cheerful countenance is said to bring good luck, and she is also known as Otafuku, which means literally "lots of luck." There is also a theory that she is Fukusuke's bride, so you could pair them together with a wish for a happy marriage.

→ 折り図 p92

おかめ
Okame

アド・ミュージアム 東京

福助、おかめ夫妻を描いた「歳徳神おかめ福助図」(部分)。

さるぼぼ
Sarubobo ★★

「ぼぼ」とは飛騨高山地方の方言で「赤ん坊」の意味。つまり、「さるぼぼ」とは「猿の赤ん坊」のことです。飛騨地方のみやげ物として人気で、「災いが去る」の語呂合わせのある縁起物です。

Bobo means "baby" in the Hida dialect of western Japan, and *saru* means monkey, so Sarubobo is literally a "monkey's baby." It is a popular souvenir from Hida, and is a popular amulet since *saru* rhymes with the phrase *wazawai ga saru*, which means "to ward off evil."

→ 折り図 p93

さるぼぼ
Sarubobo

福助
ふくすけ
Fukusuke

才槌頭にちょんまげを結い、袴姿で座る福助。絶大な人気を誇る商売の神様です。江戸時代には七福神に福助を加えて「八福神」にしようという運動までありましたが、残念ながら実現しませんでした。

Fukusuke is an enormously popular god of commerce. In the Edo period there was even a campaign to include Fukusuke in the Seven Gods of Good Fortune, making them eight gods in all, but sadly this never came about.

63　→ 折り図 p95

福助
Fukusuke

引札「大牧初三郎商店　小判を
まく福助」(部分)。

獅子舞 Shishimai → 折り紙 p17

折り図
Instructions & Diagrams

●折り図の記号や、複数の折り方に共通する「基本の折り方」は、p16を参照してください。
See p16, for an explanation of folding symbols and basic folds.

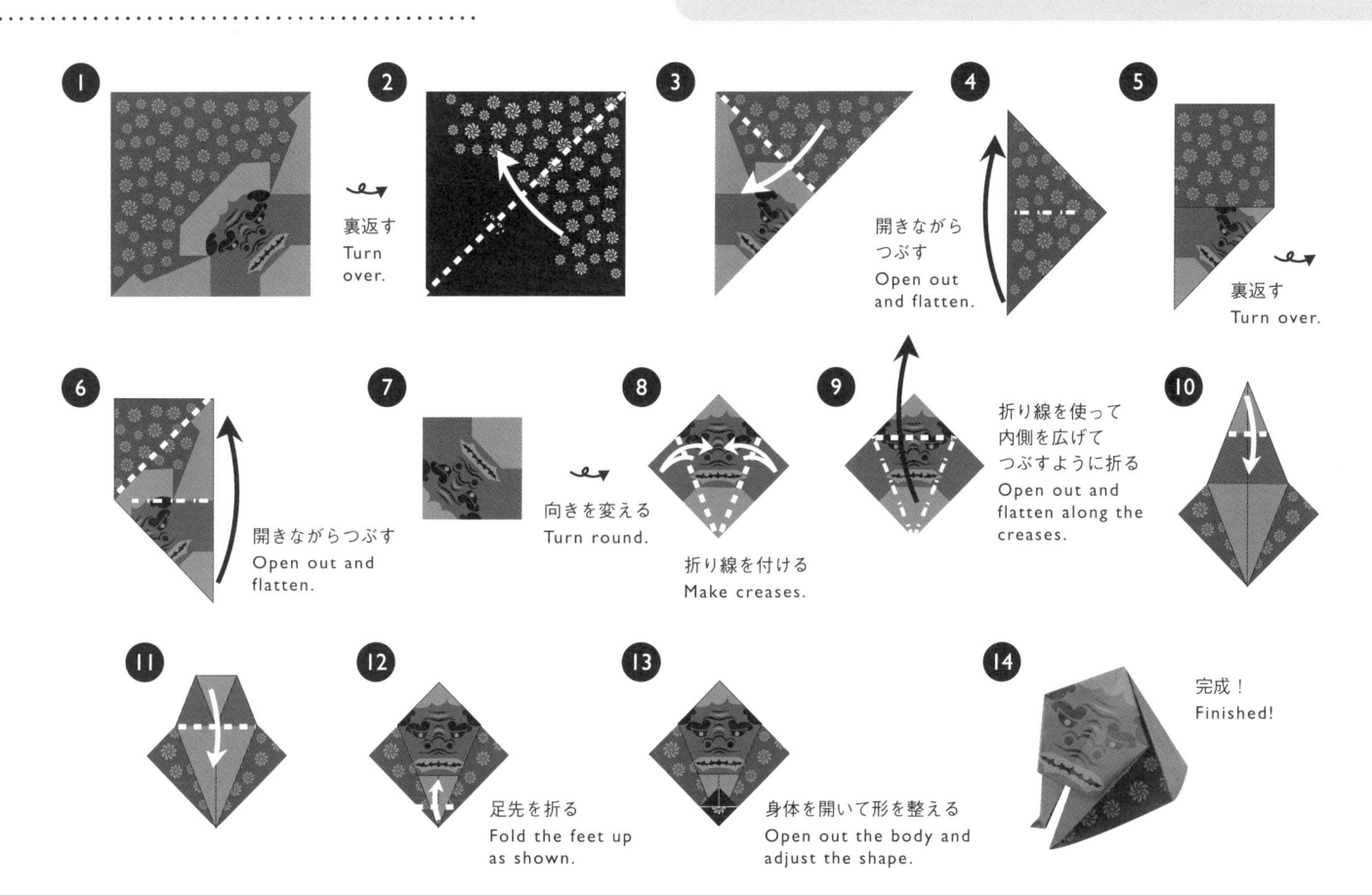

1.

2. 裏返す
Turn over.

3.

4. 開きながらつぶす
Open out and flatten.

5. 裏返す
Turn over.

6. 開きながらつぶす
Open out and flatten.

7. 向きを変える
Turn round.

8. 折り線を付ける
Make creases.

9. 折り線を使って内側を広げてつぶすように折る
Open out and flatten along the creases.

10.

11.

12. 足先を折る
Fold the feet up as shown.

13. 身体を開いて形を整える
Open out the body and adjust the shape.

14. 完成！
Finished!

★★ 招き猫 Maneki-Neko → 折り紙 p19

1

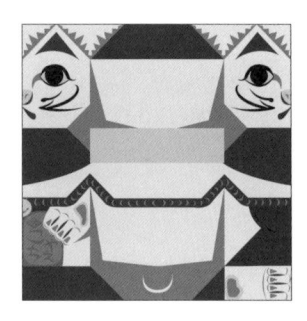

2 裏返す
Turn over.

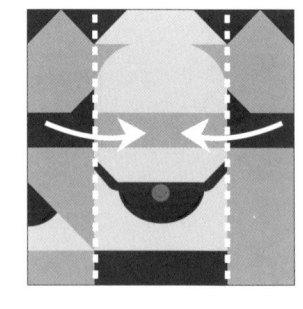

3  折り線を付ける
Make a crease.

4 折り線を使って開きながらつぶす
Open out and flatten along the crease.

5 4と同じように開きながらつぶす
Repeat on the other side.

6

7 裏返す
Turn over.

8 開きながらつぶす
Open out and flatten.

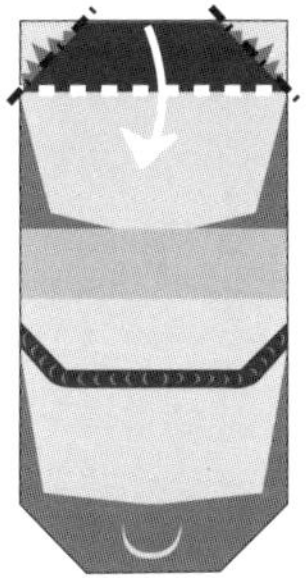

9

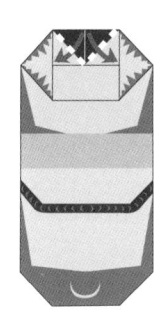

10

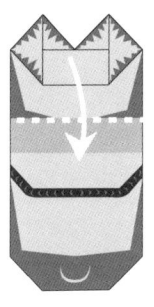

11

12 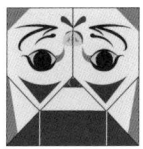 裏返す
Turn over.

13

14  後ろの顔を起こしながら谷折り
Make a valley fold to bring the face up from behind.

15 完成！
Finished!

✱✱ 鶴 Crane → 折り紙 p21

①

② 裏返す
Turn over.

③ 折り線を付ける
Make a crease.

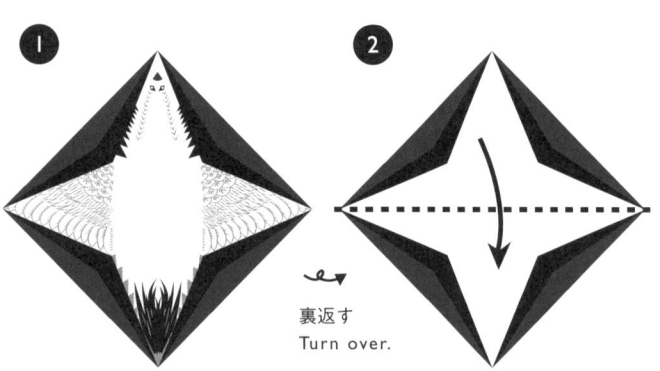

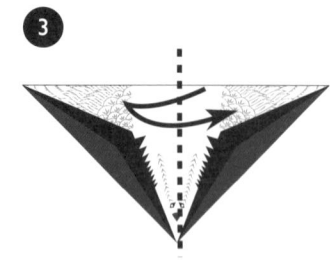

④ 折り線を使って○と○を合わせるように開きながらつぶす
Open out along the crease and then fold over so the two circles meet.

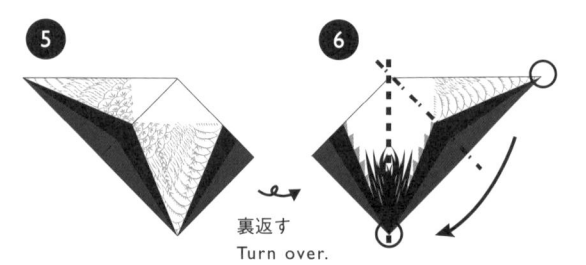

⑤ 裏返す
Turn over.

⑥ 4と同じように開きながらつぶす
Repeat step 4 as shown.

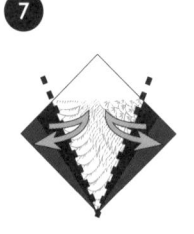

⑦ 折り線を付ける
Make creases.

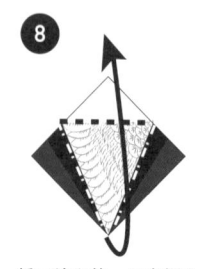

⑧ 折り線を使って内側を広げてつぶすように折る
Open out and flatten along the creases.

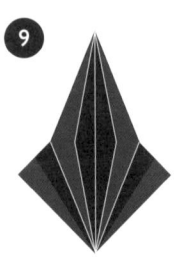

⑨ 裏返して7、8と同じように折る
Turn over and repeat steps 7 and 8.

68

⑩

⑪
裏返して10と 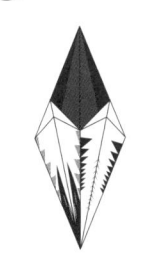
同じように折る
Turn over and fold
as in step 10.

⑫ 
1枚めくって違う面を出す
(裏も同様に)
Fold over the top flap to
reveal a new surface.
Repeat on the other side.

⑬ 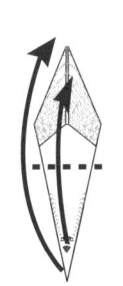
谷折りで折り上げる
(裏も同様に)
Fold up using a valley
fold. Repeat on the
other side.

⑭ 
1枚めくって違う面を出す
(裏も同様に)
Fold over the top flap to
reveal a new surface.
Repeat on the other side.

⑮ 
頭と尾を引き出す
Pull out the head
and tail.

⑯ 
「中割り折り」(→p16)で
くちばしを作る
Use an inside reverse
fold to make the beak.

⑰ 
○部分をもって羽を広げる
Holding the tips marked
○, pull out the wings as
shown.

⑱
完成！
Finished!

69

亀 Turtle → 折り紙 p23

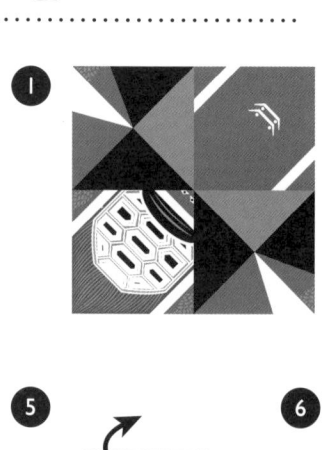

1.
2. 裏返す
   Turn over.
3. 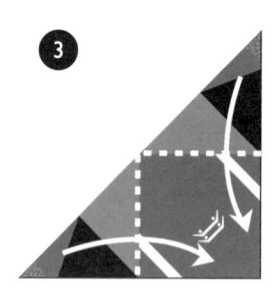
4.  上の1組のみ谷折り。
   Fold over the top flaps as shown.
5. 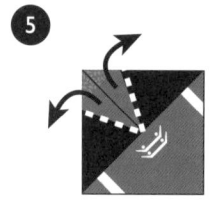
6. 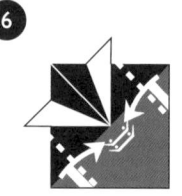
7. 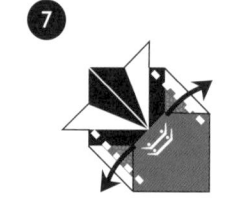
8.
9. 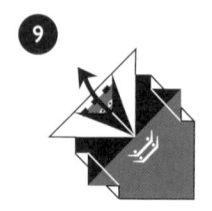
10.  裏返す
    Turn over.
11. 軽く山折り
    Make a slight mountain fold.
12. 完成！
    Finished!

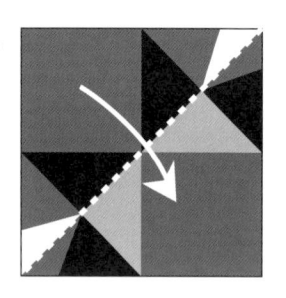

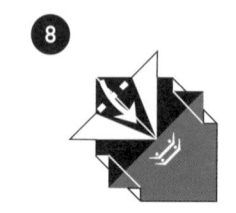

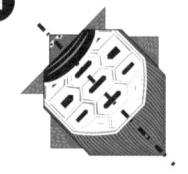

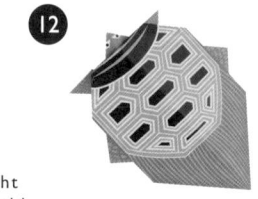

70

姫だるま Hime-Daruma → 折り紙 p25

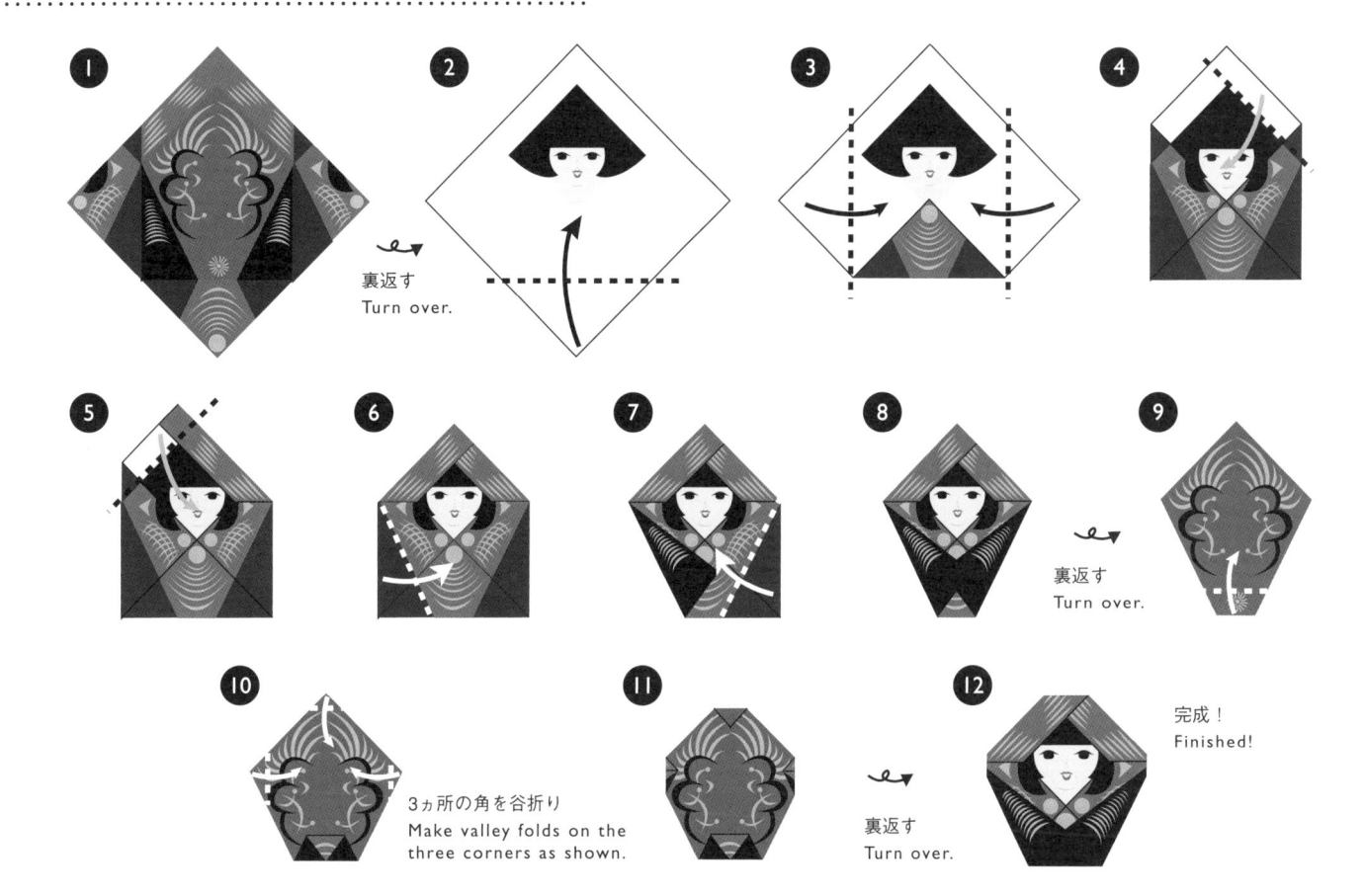

①

② 裏返す
Turn over.

③

④

⑤

⑥

⑦

⑧ 裏返す
Turn over.

⑨

⑩ 3ヵ所の角を谷折り
Make valley folds on the three corners as shown.

⑪

⑫ 裏返す
Turn over.

完成！
Finished!

★ うさぎ Rabbit → 折り紙 p27

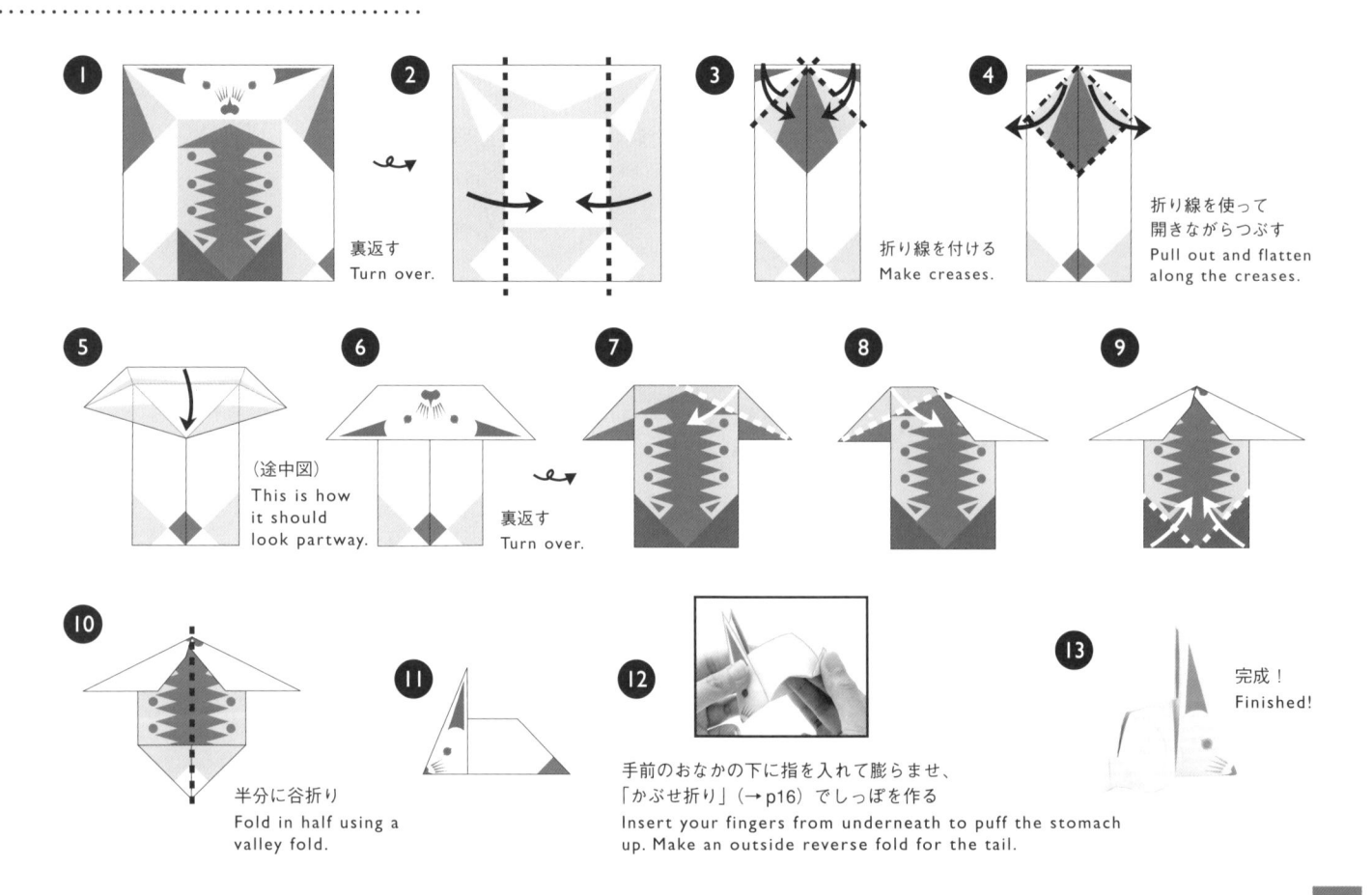

1

2 裏返す
Turn over.

3 折り線を付ける
Make creases.

4 折り線を使って開きながらつぶす
Pull out and flatten along the creases.

5

6 (途中図) This is how it should look partway. 裏返す Turn over.

7

8

9

10 半分に谷折り
Fold in half using a valley fold.

11

12 手前のおなかの下に指を入れて膨らませ、「かぶせ折り」(→p16) でしっぽを作る
Insert your fingers from underneath to puff the stomach up. Make an outside reverse fold for the tail.

13 完成！
Finished!

海老 Lobster → 折り紙 p29

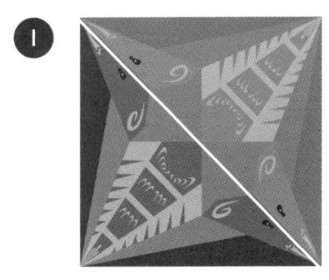

1 ハサミで半分に切る
Cut in half with scissors.

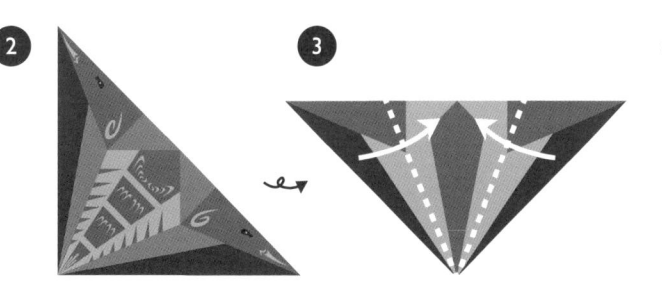

2 裏返し、向きを変える
Turn over and around as shown.

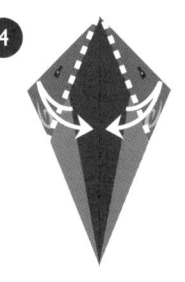

3

4 折り線を付ける
Make creases.

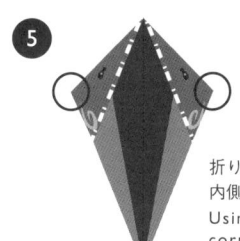

5 折り線を使って○の部分を内側へ折り込む
Using the creases, fold in the corners marked ○.

6 （途中図）
This is how it should look partway.

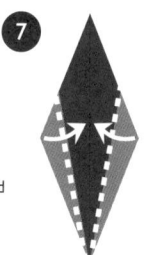

7

8

9

10 半分に谷折り
Fold in half using a valley fold.

11 しっぽの方から山折り、谷折りを繰り返し、形を整える
Starting from the tail, make stair folds as shown, and adjust the shape.

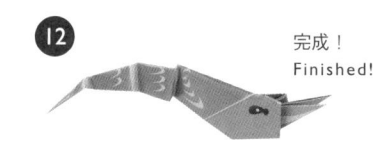

12 完成！
Finished!

おしどり「雄」 Mandarin Drake → 折り紙 p31

1

2 裏返す
Turn over.

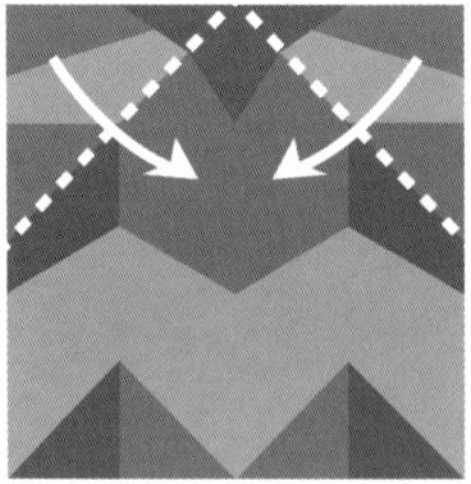

3

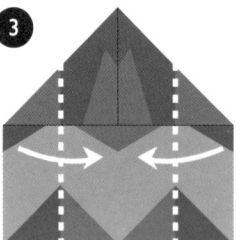

4  折り線を付ける
Make a crease.

5 折り線を使って開きながらつぶす
Open out and flatten along the crease.

6

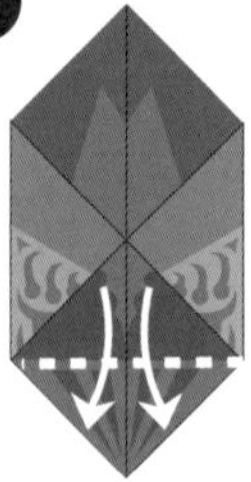

7  裏返す
Turn over.

8 折り線を付ける
Make creases.

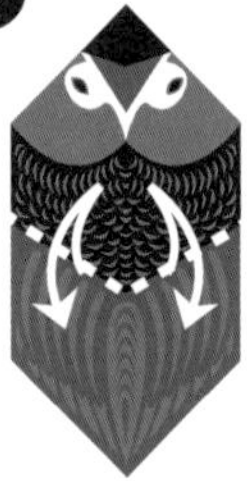

9 折り線を付ける
Make a crease.

10 8、9で付けた折り線を使って立体的にする
Use the creases made in steps 8 and 9 to make up the body as shown.

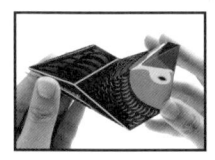

11 「中割り折り」(→p16)
Make an inside reverse fold.

12 完成！
Finished!

おしどり「雌」 Mandarin Duck → 折り紙 p33

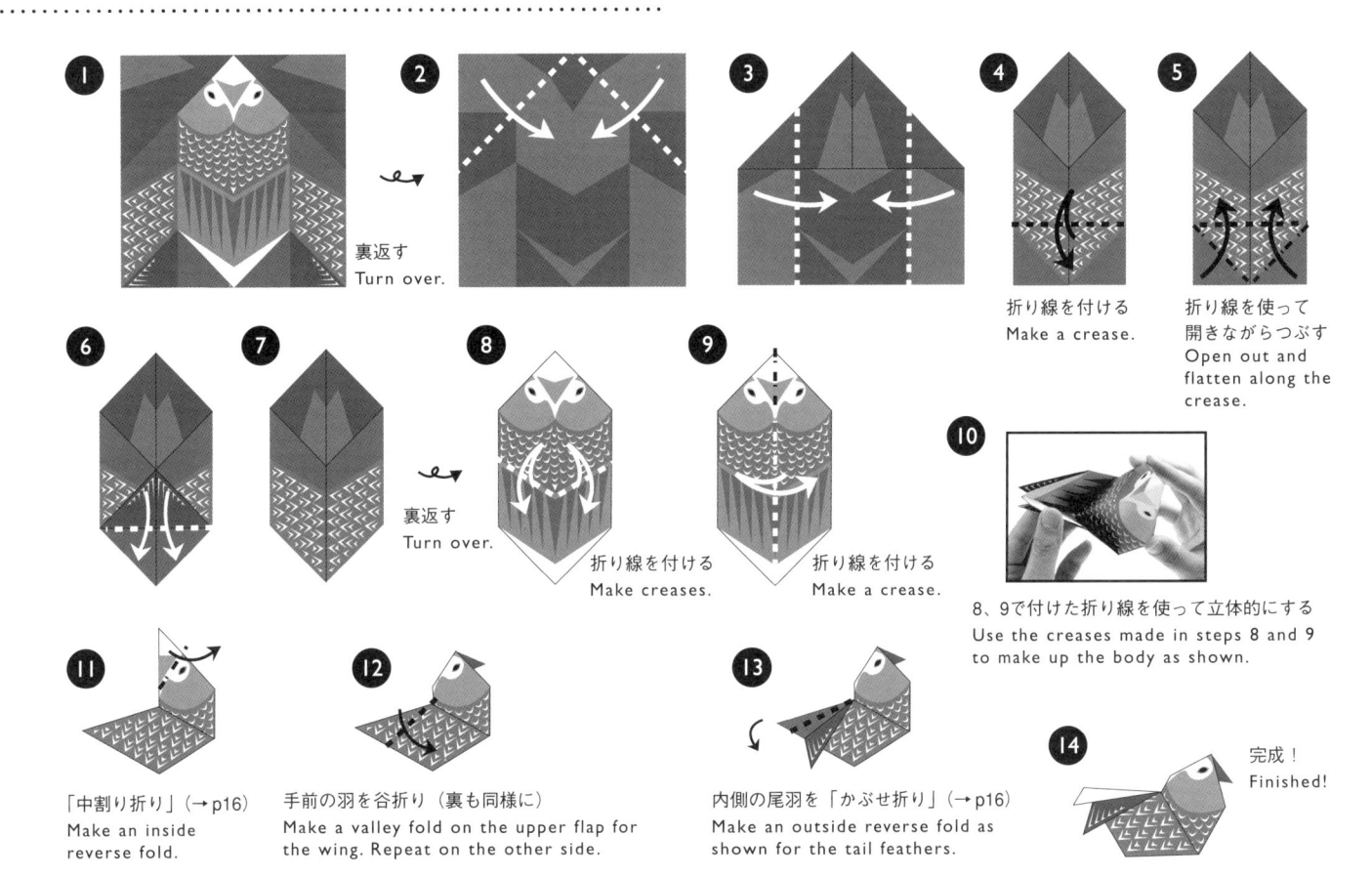

① 裏返す Turn over.

②

③

④ 折り線を付ける Make a crease.

⑤ 折り線を使って開きながらつぶす Open out and flatten along the crease.

⑥

⑦ 裏返す Turn over.

⑧ 折り線を付ける Make creases.

⑨ 折り線を付ける Make a crease.

⑩ 8、9で付けた折り線を使って立体的にする Use the creases made in steps 8 and 9 to make up the body as shown.

⑪ 「中割り折り」(→p16) Make an inside reverse fold.

⑫ 手前の羽を谷折り（裏も同様に） Make a valley fold on the upper flap for the wing. Repeat on the other side.

⑬ 内側の尾羽を「かぶせ折り」(→p16) Make an outside reverse fold as shown for the tail feathers.

⑭ 完成！ Finished!

ご祝儀袋 Goshūgi-bukuro → 折り紙 p35

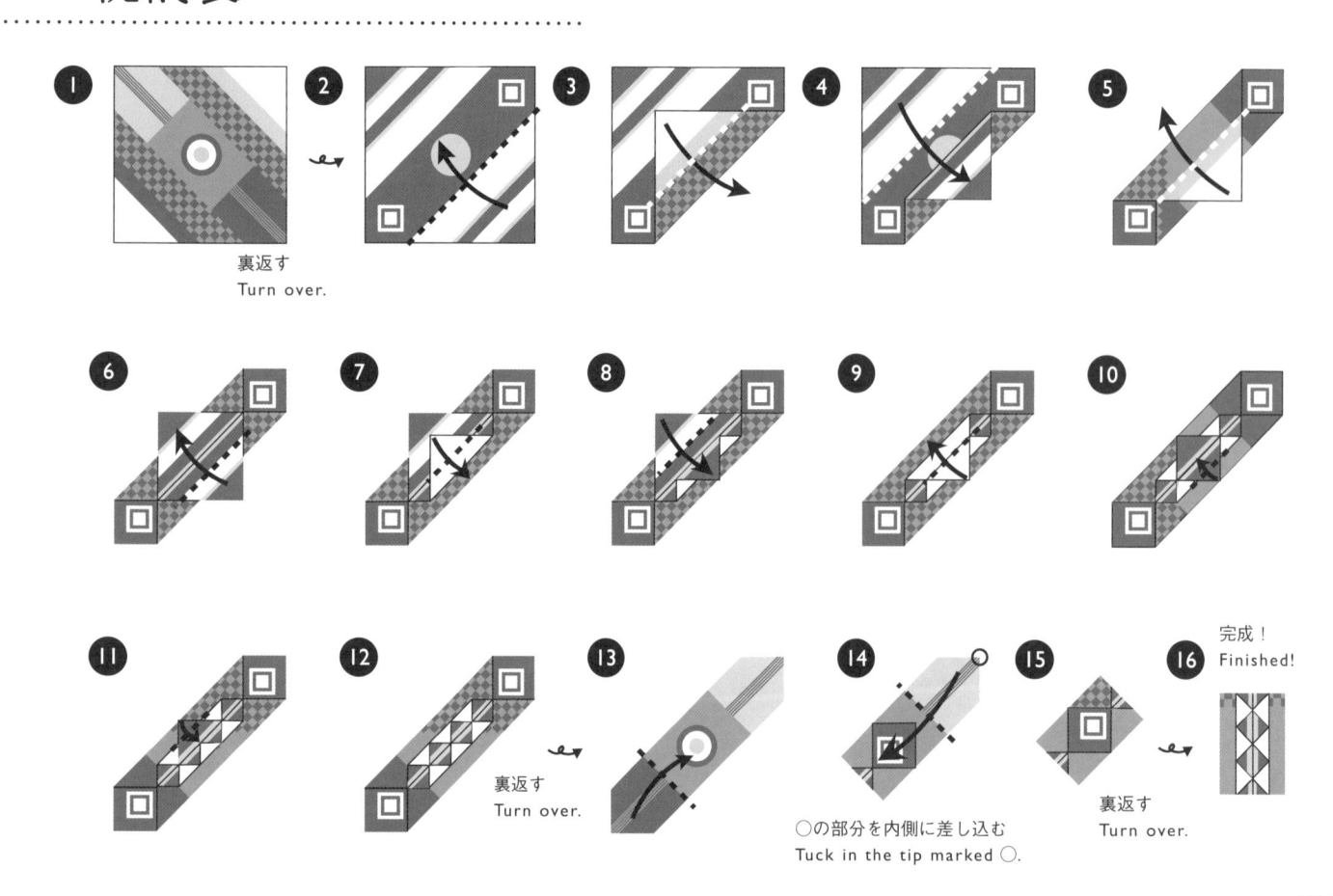

1.
2. 裏返す / Turn over.
3.
4.
5.
6.
7.
8.
9.
10.
11.
12. 裏返す / Turn over.
13.
14. ○の部分を内側に差し込む / Tuck in the tip marked ○.
15. 裏返す / Turn over.
16. 完成！/ Finished!

76

★ かえる Frog → 折り紙 p37

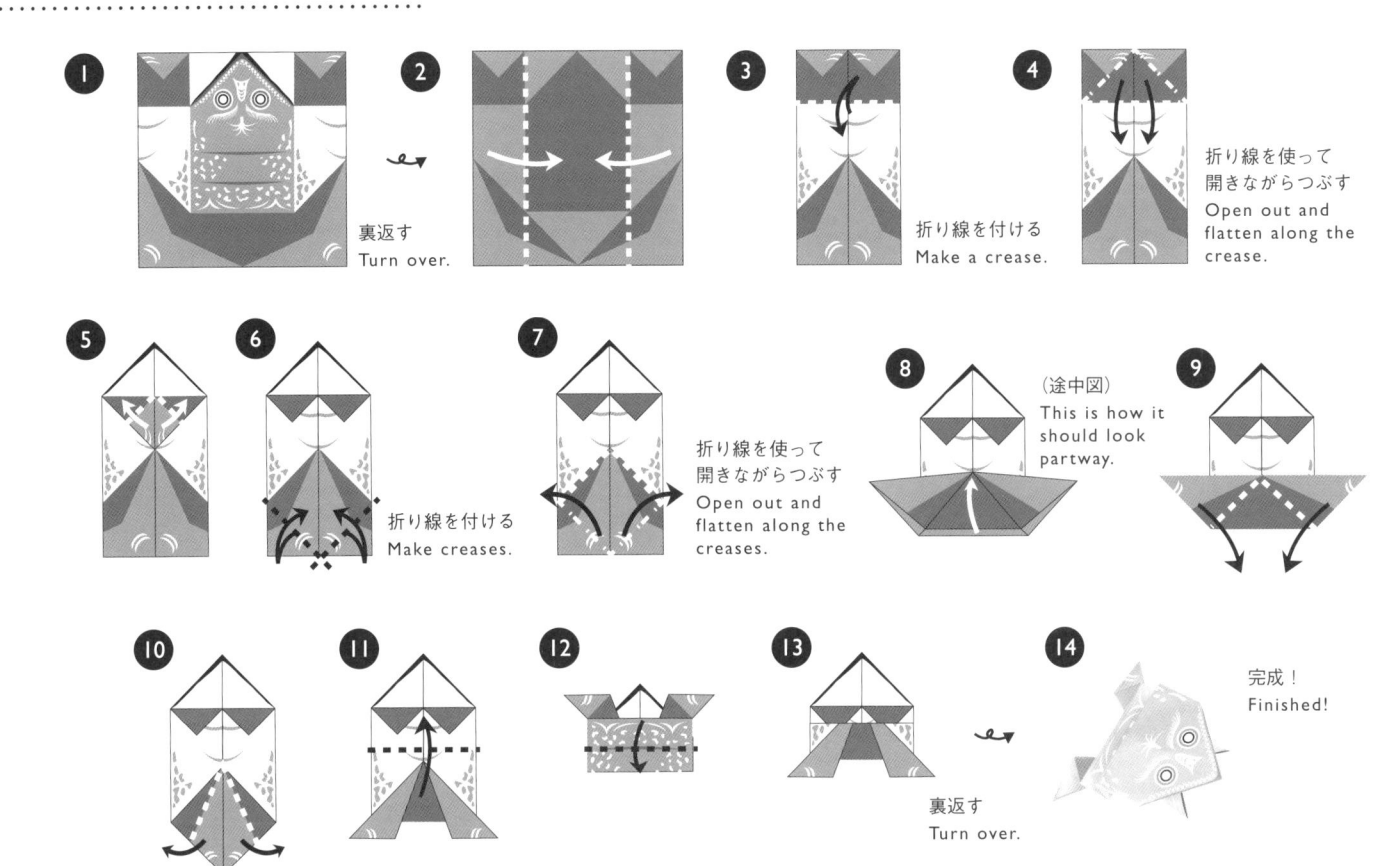

1

2 裏返す
Turn over.

3 折り線を付ける
Make a crease.

4 折り線を使って開きながらつぶす
Open out and flatten along the crease.

5

6 折り線を付ける
Make creases.

7 折り線を使って開きながらつぶす
Open out and flatten along the creases.

8 （途中図）
This is how it should look partway.

9

10

11

12

13 裏返す
Turn over.

14 完成！
Finished!

お狐さま Okitsune-sama → 折り紙 p39

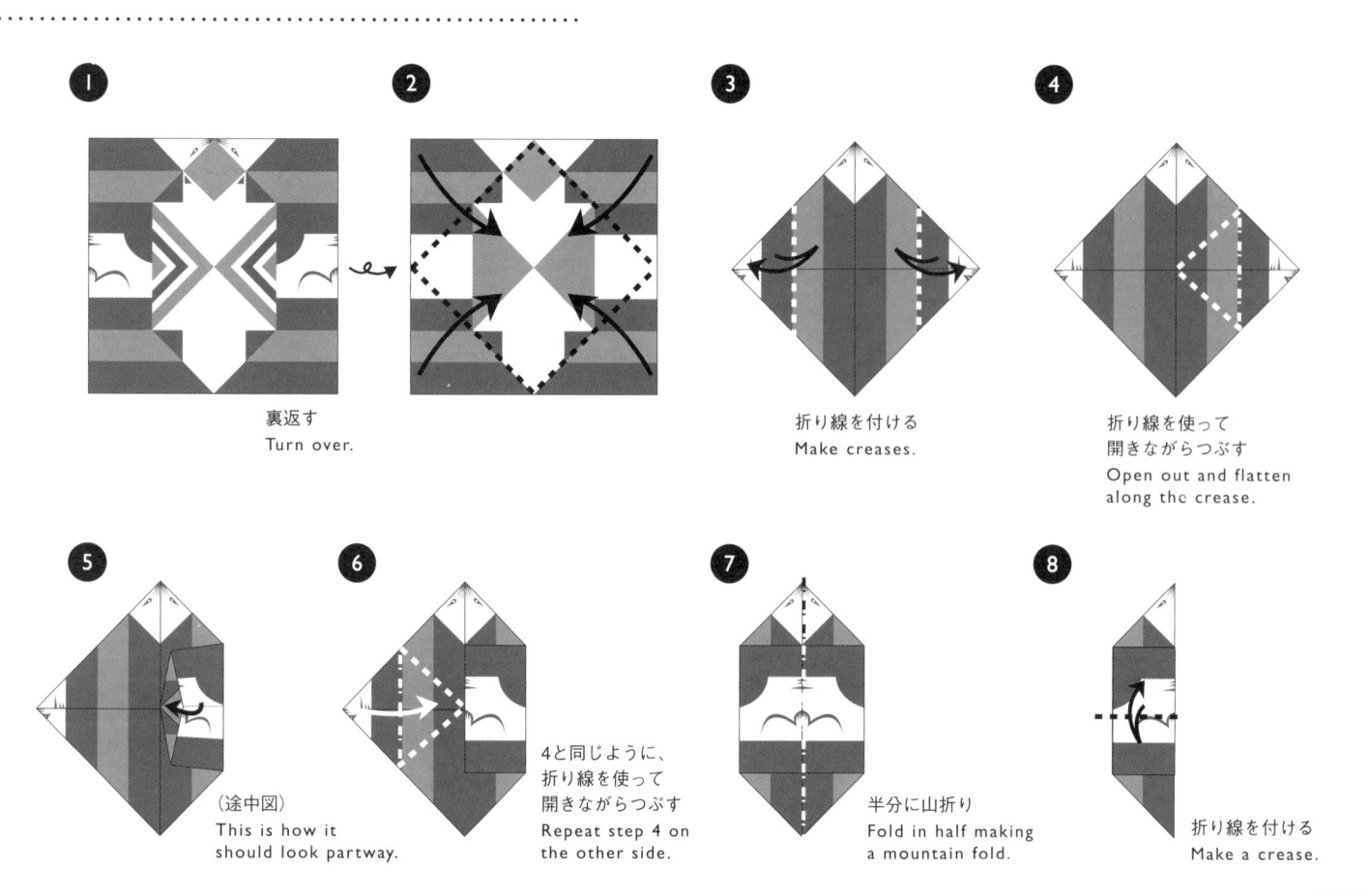

1

2
裏返す
Turn over.

3
折り線を付ける
Make creases.

4
折り線を使って開きながらつぶす
Open out and flatten along the crease.

5
（途中図）
This is how it should look partway.

6
4と同じように、折り線を使って開きながらつぶす
Repeat step 4 on the other side.

7
半分に山折り
Fold in half making a mountain fold.

8
折り線を付ける
Make a crease.

78

9

◎の内側を開きながら、折り線を使って○と合わせるようにつぶす
Open out along the crease and then fold over so the two circles meet.

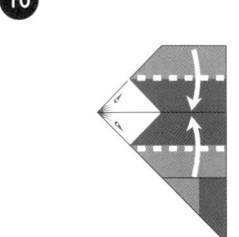

10

つぶしたところ
This is how it should look.

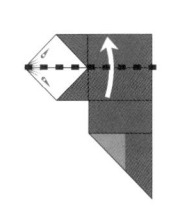

11

上の一組を谷折り
Make a valley fold on the top flap.

12

9と同じように折り線を使って○の内側を開きながらつぶす
As in step 9, open out along the crease and fold over.

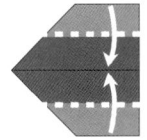

13

つぶしたところ
This is how it should look.

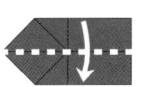

14

15

中割り折り
Make an inside reverse fold.

16

向きを変える
Turn round.

完成！
Finished!

79

★★★
恵比寿 Ebisu → 折り紙 p43

1

2 裏返す Turn over.

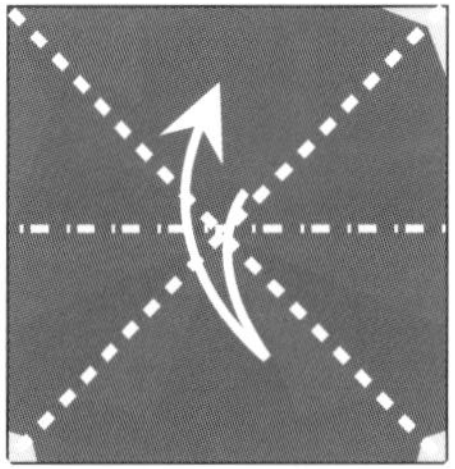

横、斜めに折り線を付ける
Make horizontal and diagonal creases as shown.

3 裏返す Turn over.

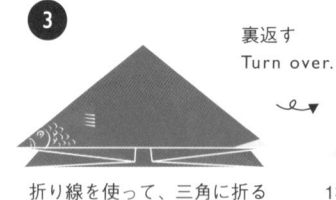

折り線を使って、三角に折る
Use the creases to make a triangular form.

4

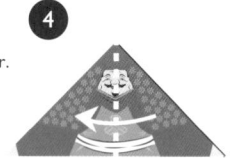

1枚めくって違う面を出す
Turn over the top flap to reveal a different surface.

5

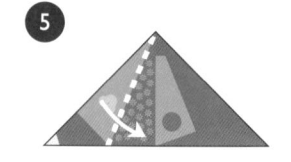

6

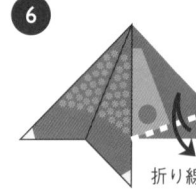

折り線を付ける
Make a crease.

7

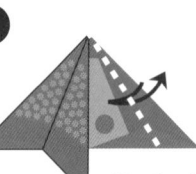

折り線を付ける
Make a crease.

8

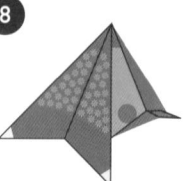

6、7の折り線を使って
つまむように折り下げる
Fold pinching together the creases made in steps 6 and 7.

9

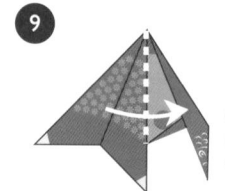

2組谷折りで右に倒す
Fold over two flaps using a valley fold.

10

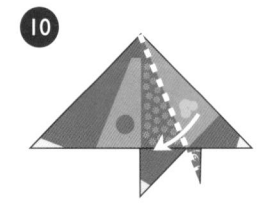

11

12

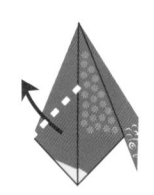

13 1組谷折りで左に倒す
Fold over one flap using a valley fold.

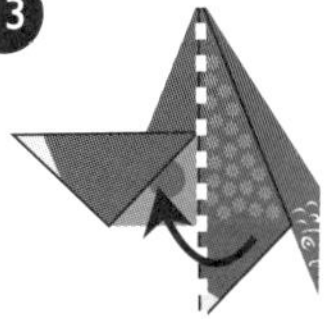

14 手を軽く谷折り
Make a slight valley fold for the hand.

15

16  裏返す
Turn over.

17

18

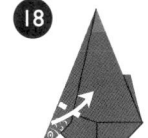

19

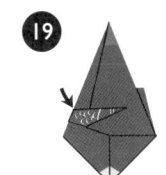

20  19の矢印部分（鯛）を開き、ややつぶしながら後ろにまわす
Open out the fish, and bring it back, gently flattening it.

裏返す
Turn over.

21 鯛の口を谷折り
Make a valley fold on the mouth of the fish.

22 烏帽子を「段折り」（→p16）
Make a stair fold on the hat.

23

24  左足の先を山折り
Make a mountain fold on his left foot.

25 足を90°下げてから、重ねて足先を引っ掛け、手を鯛の口先に差し込む
Cross the legs over and fix in place, then tuck the hand into the fish.

26 完成！
Finished!

大黒天 Daikokuten → 折り紙 p45

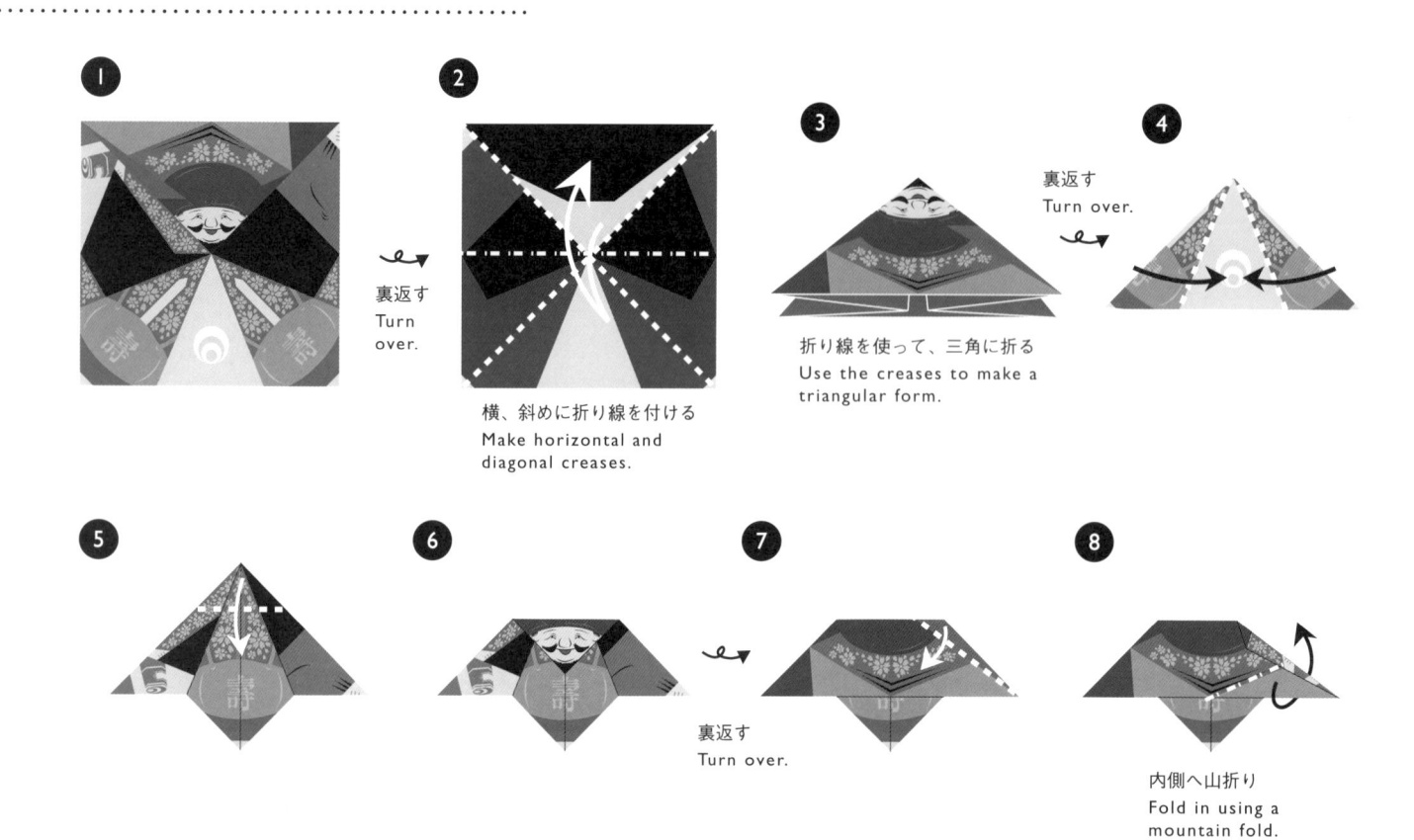

1.

2. 裏返す
Turn over.

横、斜めに折り線を付ける
Make horizontal and diagonal creases.

3. 折り線を使って、三角に折る
Use the creases to make a triangular form.

4. 裏返す
Turn over.

5.

6.

7. 裏返す
Turn over.

8. 内側へ山折り
Fold in using a mountain fold.

82

9

10

裏返す
Turn over.

11

「段折り」(→p16)
Make a stair fold.

12

腕を谷折り
（頭部は折らない）
Make a valley fold in the arm, taking care not to fold the head.

13

14

15

少し山折り
Make a slight mountain fold.

16

17

右足の先を山折り
Make a mountain fold on his right foot.

18

足を90°下げ、重ねて足先を引っ掛ける
Cross the legs over and fix in place.

19

完成！
Finished!

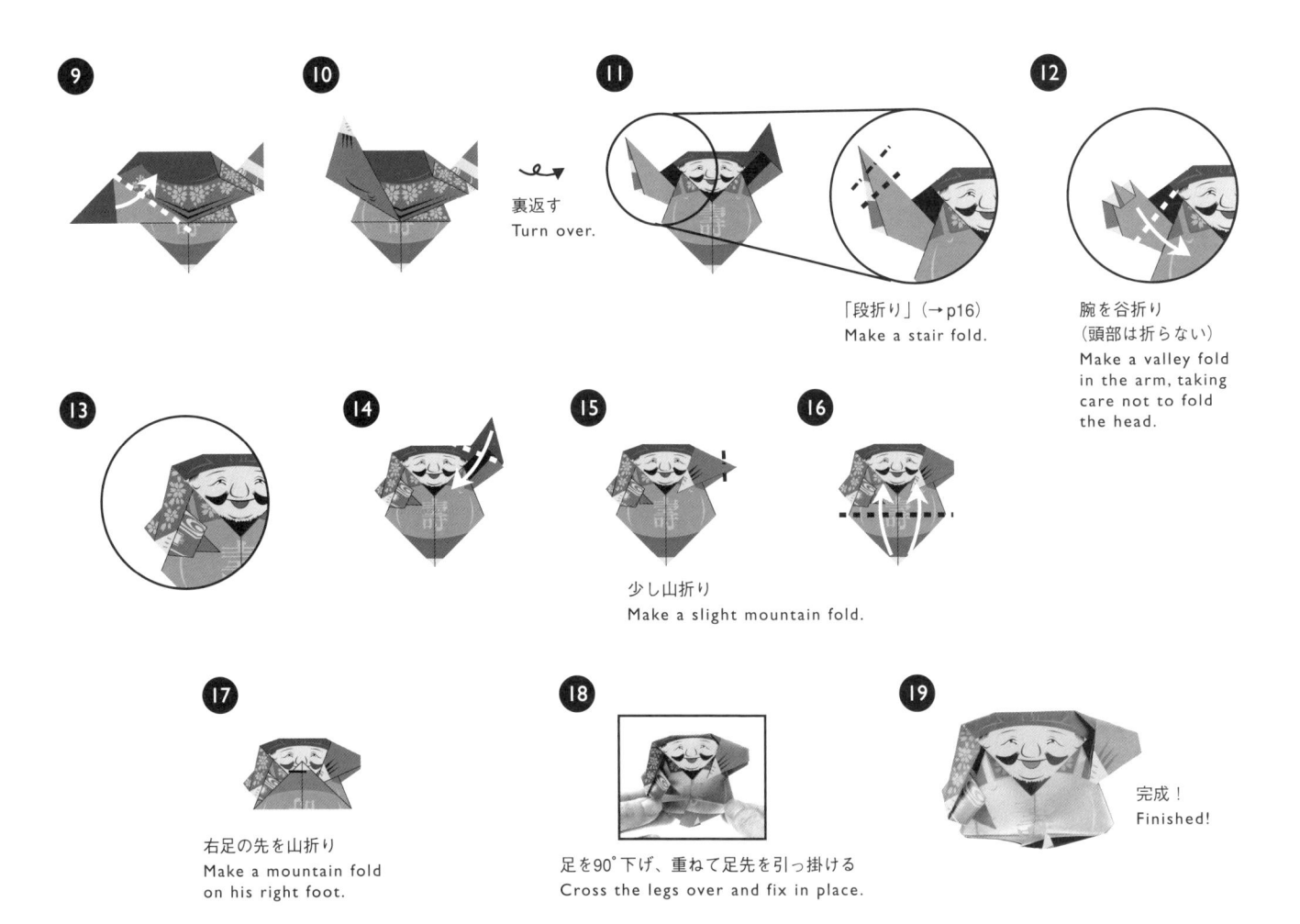

福禄寿 Fukurokuju → 折り紙 p47

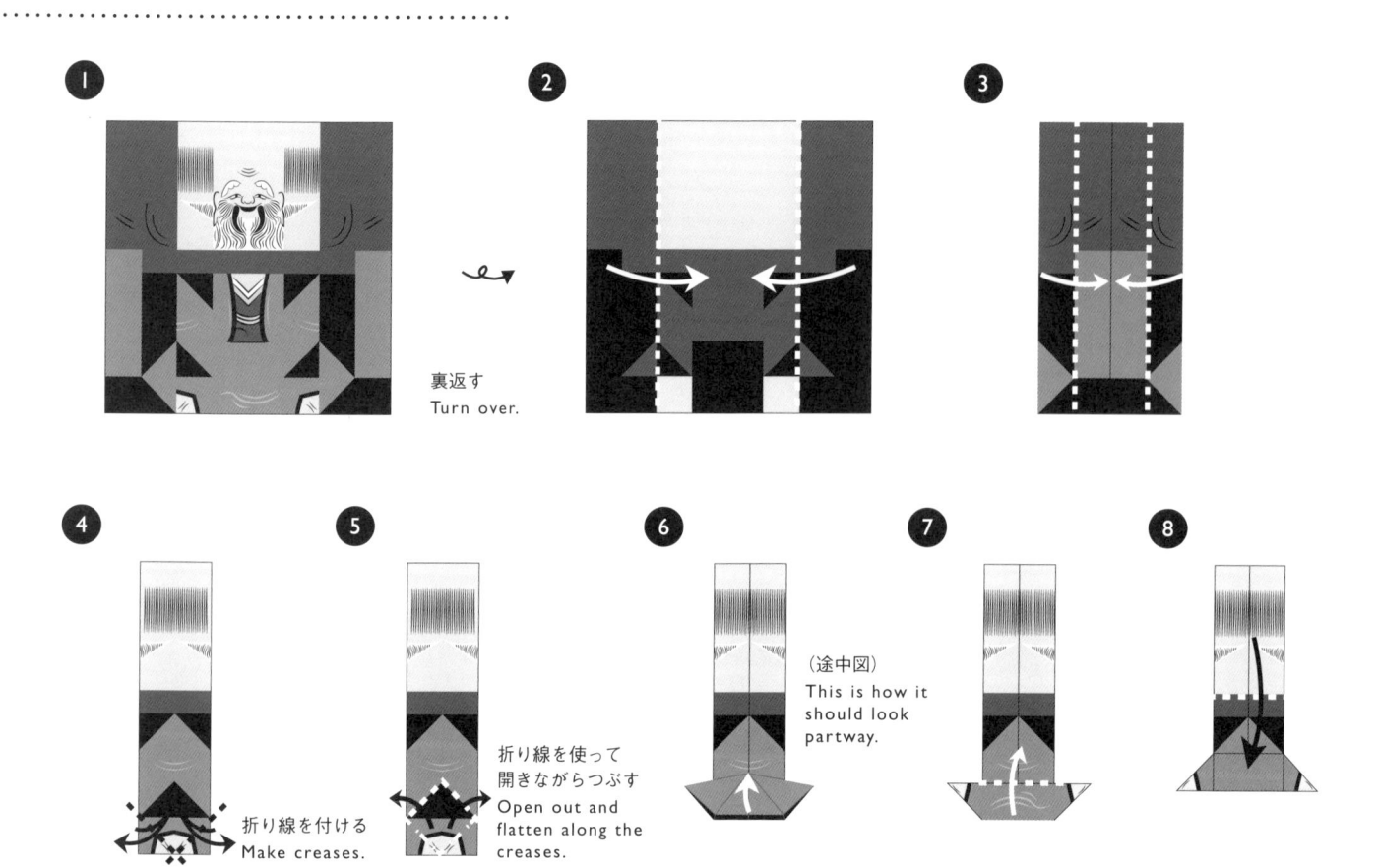

1

2 裏返す
Turn over.

3

4 折り線を付ける
Make creases.

5 折り線を使って開きながらつぶす
Open out and flatten along the creases.

6

7 （途中図）
This is how it should look partway.

8

84

9

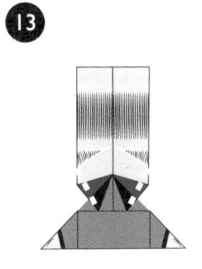

10 裏返す
Turn over.

谷折りしながら顔を起こす
Make a valley fold to bring the head up as shown.

11

12 裏返す
Turn over.

→部分を開きながらつぶす
Open out the parts indicated by the arrows, and flatten.

13 少し谷折り
Make slight valley folds.

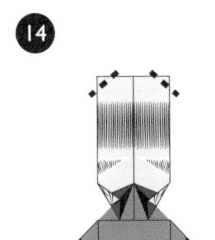

14 頭を少し谷折り
Make slight valley folds as shown.

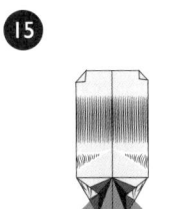

15 裏返す
Turn over.

16

17 体を起こし、手先を山折り
Pull out the head, and make mountain folds for the hands.

18 完成！
Finished!

★ 扇子 Sensu → 折り紙 p41

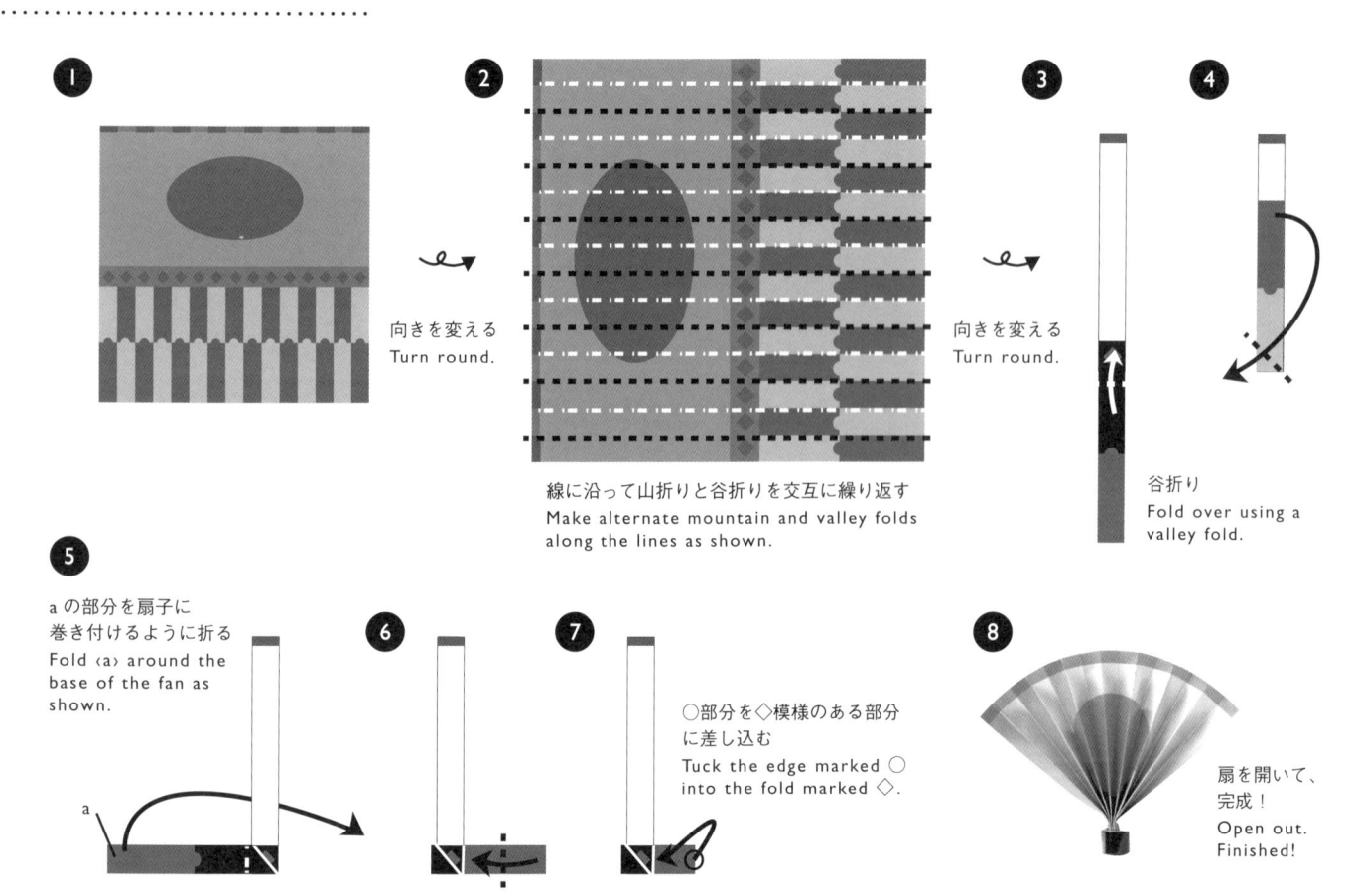

1

2

向きを変える
Turn round.

線に沿って山折りと谷折りを交互に繰り返す
Make alternate mountain and valley folds along the lines as shown.

3

向きを変える
Turn round.

4

谷折り
Fold over using a valley fold.

5

a の部分を扇子に巻き付けるように折る
Fold ‹a› around the base of the fan as shown.

6

7

○部分を◇模様のある部分に差し込む
Tuck the edge marked ○ into the fold marked ◇.

8

扇を開いて、完成！
Open out. Finished!

86

★ 布袋、毘沙門天、寿老人、弁財天 Hotei, Bishamonten, Jurōjin, Benzaiten →折り紙 p49

1

2 裏返す Turn over.

3 「段折り」(→p16) Make a stair fold.

↓部分を開きながらつぶす
Open out the part indicated by the arrow, and flatten.

4

5 ○の2ヵ所も2、3と同じように折る
Repeat steps 2 and 3 in the places marked ○.

6 「段折り」 Make a stair fold.

7

8

9

10

11 7、8、9で折った部分を少し広げ、7で折った部分を首に引っ掛ける
Lightly spread the parts folded in steps 7, 8 and 9, and fix the fold made in 7 in place.

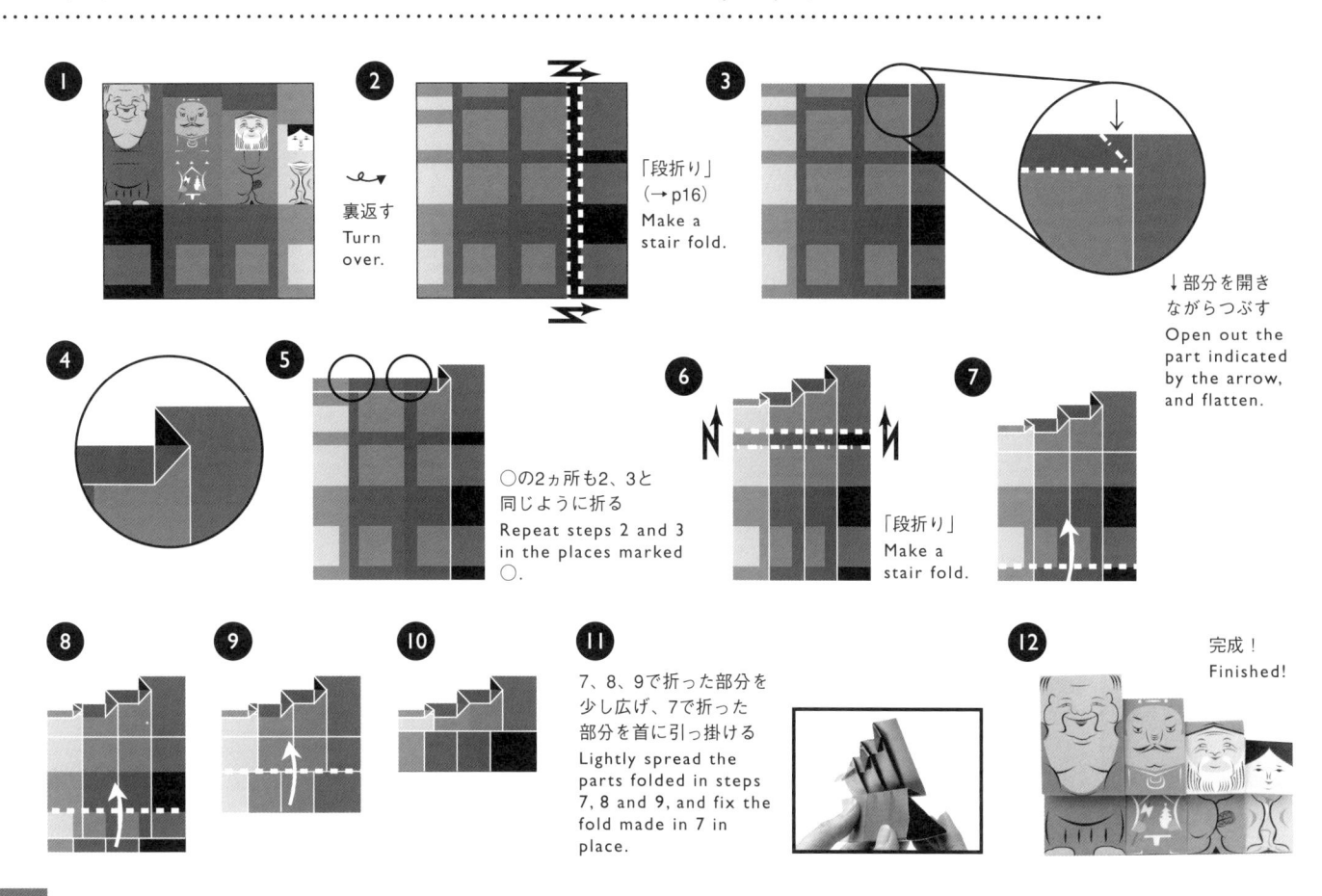

12 完成！ Finished!

★富士山 Mount Fuji → 折り紙 p51

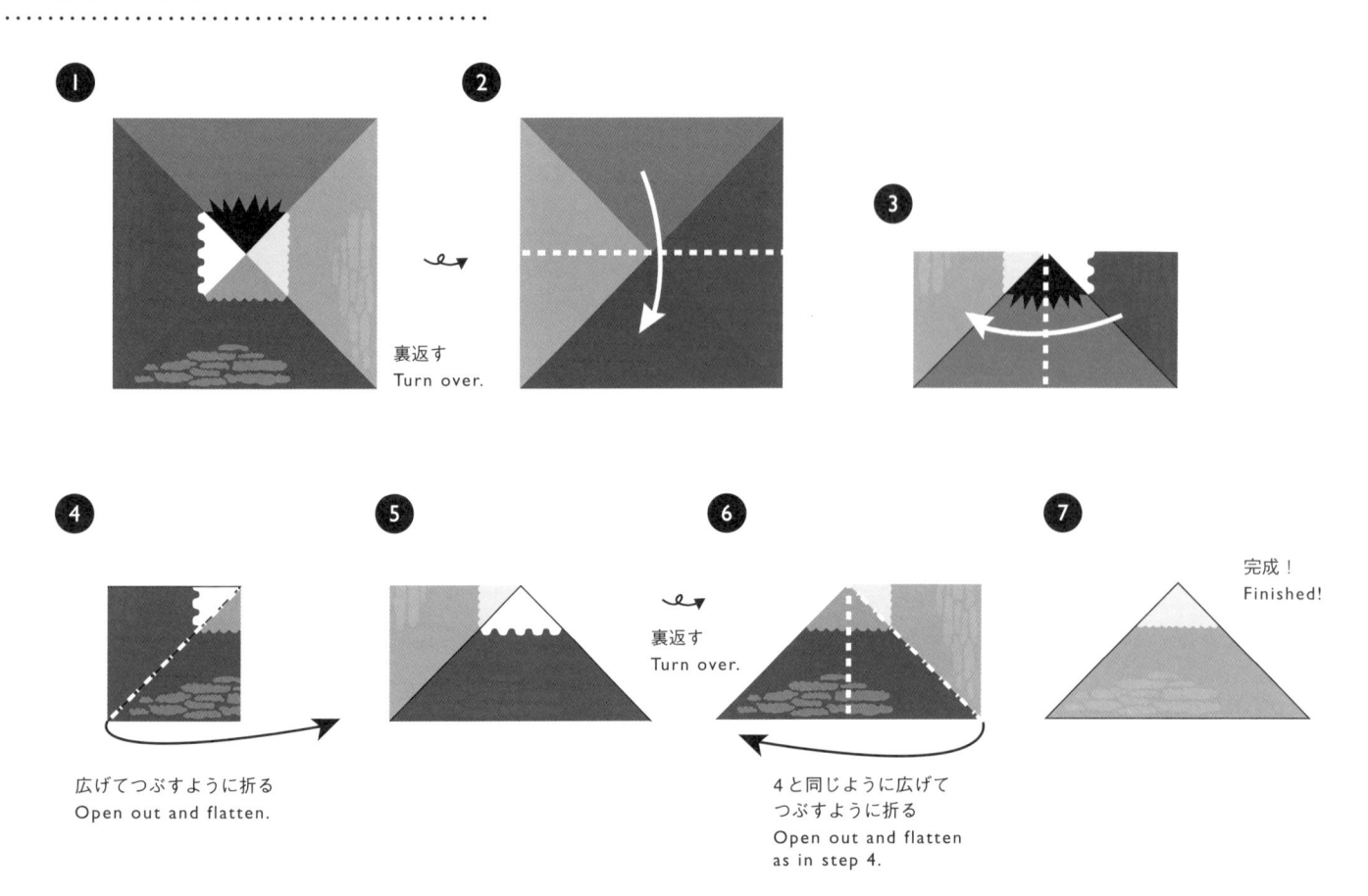

①

② 裏返す
Turn over.

③

④ 広げてつぶすように折る
Open out and flatten.

⑤ 裏返す
Turn over.

⑥ 4と同じように広げて
つぶすように折る
Open out and flatten
as in step 4.

⑦ 完成！
Finished!

こけし Kokeshi Doll → 折り紙 p53

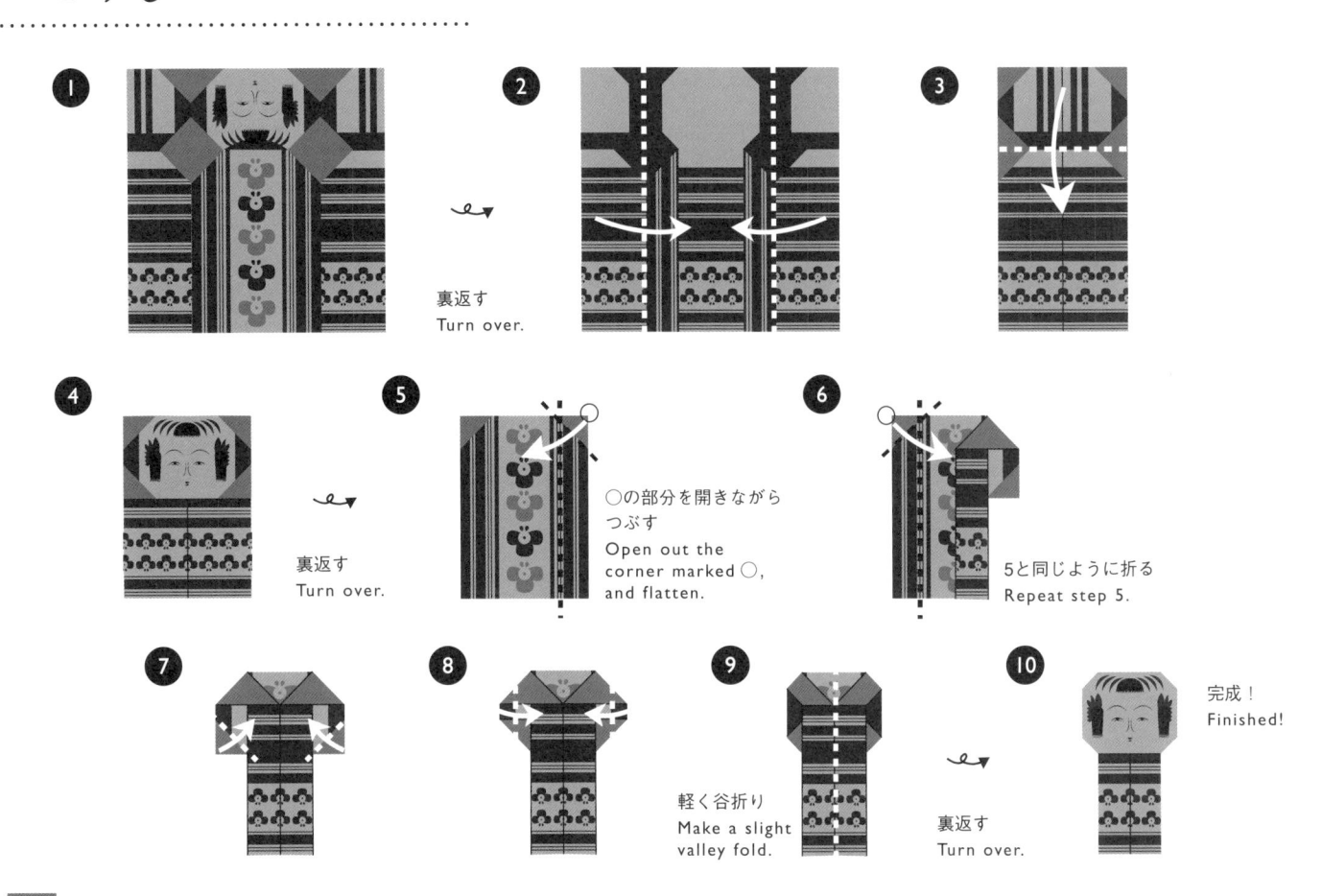

1.

2. 裏返す
Turn over.

3.

4. 裏返す
Turn over.

5. ○の部分を開きながらつぶす
Open out the corner marked ○, and flatten.

6. 5と同じように折る
Repeat step 5.

7.

8.

9. 軽く谷折り
Make a slight valley fold.

10. 裏返す
Turn over.

完成！
Finished!

兜 Warrior's Helmet → 折り紙 p55

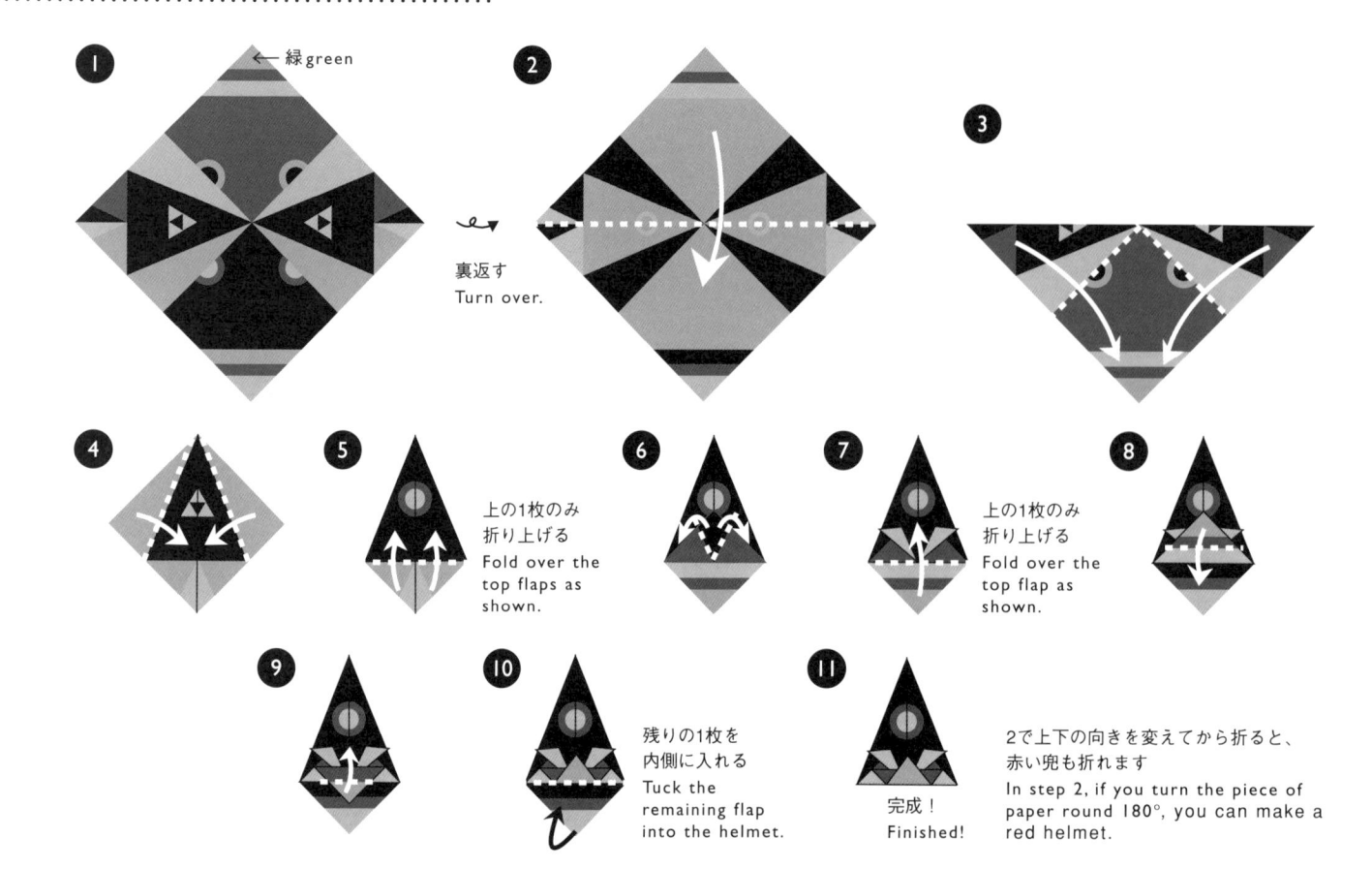

1. ← 緑 green

2. 裏返す / Turn over.

3.

4.

5. 上の1枚のみ折り上げる / Fold over the top flaps as shown.

6.

7. 上の1枚のみ折り上げる / Fold over the top flap as shown.

8.

9.

10. 残りの1枚を内側に入れる / Tuck the remaining flap into the helmet.

11. 完成！ / Finished!

2で上下の向きを変えてから折ると、赤い兜も折れます
In step 2, if you turn the piece of paper round 180°, you can make a red helmet.

★ 鯛 Sea Bream → 折り紙 p57

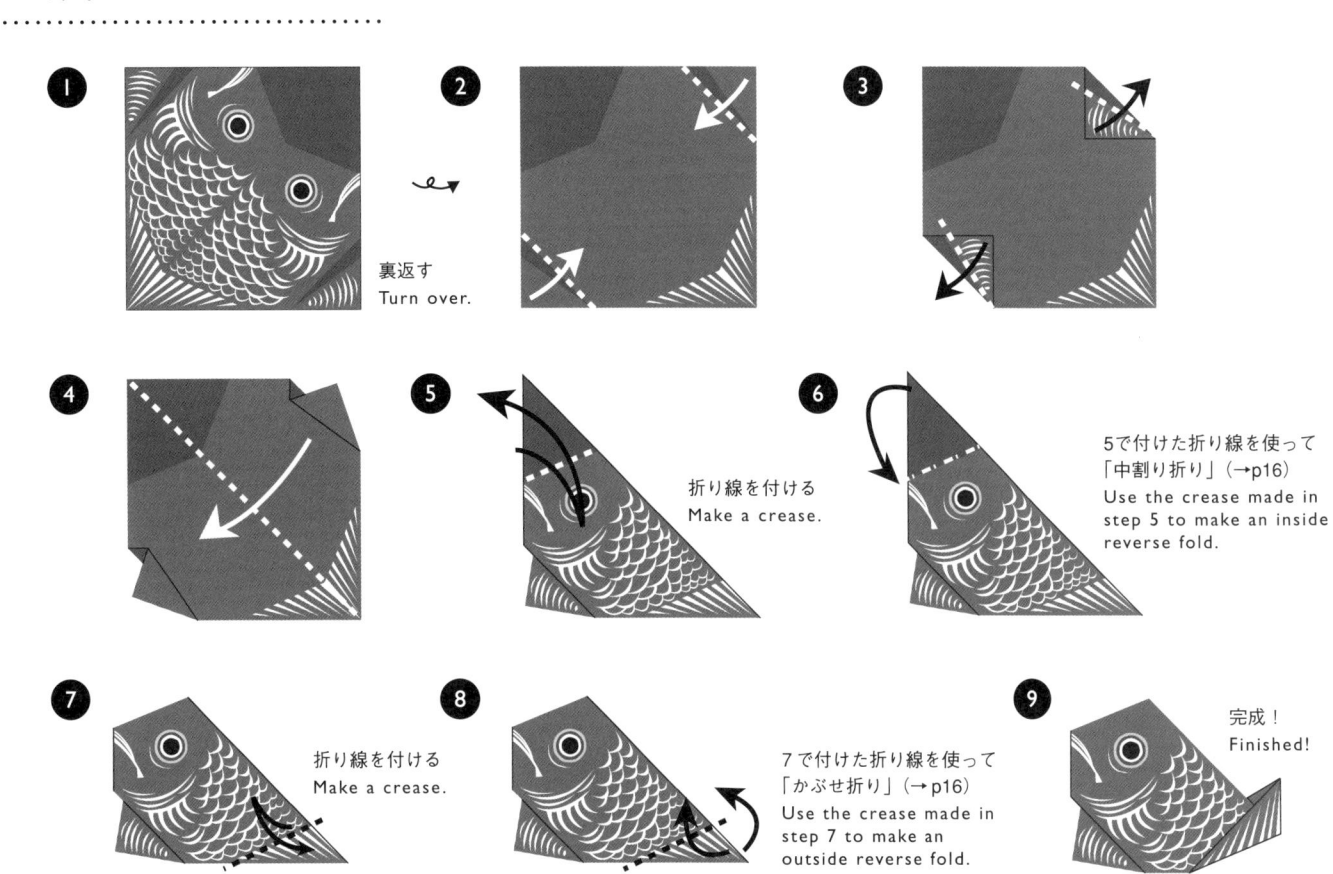

①

② 裏返す
Turn over.

③

④

⑤ 折り線を付ける
Make a crease.

⑥ 5で付けた折り線を使って
「中割り折り」(→p16)
Use the crease made in step 5 to make an inside reverse fold.

⑦ 折り線を付ける
Make a crease.

⑧ 7で付けた折り線を使って
「かぶせ折り」(→p16)
Use the crease made in step 7 to make an outside reverse fold.

⑨ 完成！
Finished!

おかめ Okame → 折り紙 p59

①

② 裏返す Turn over.

③

④ 裏返す Turn over.

⑤

⑥

⑦

⑧ 裏返す Turn over.

⑨ 2枚まとめて折る Fold over both flaps on each side.

⑩

⑪ 裏返す Turn over.

完成！ Finished!

さるぼぼ Sarubobo → 折り紙 p61

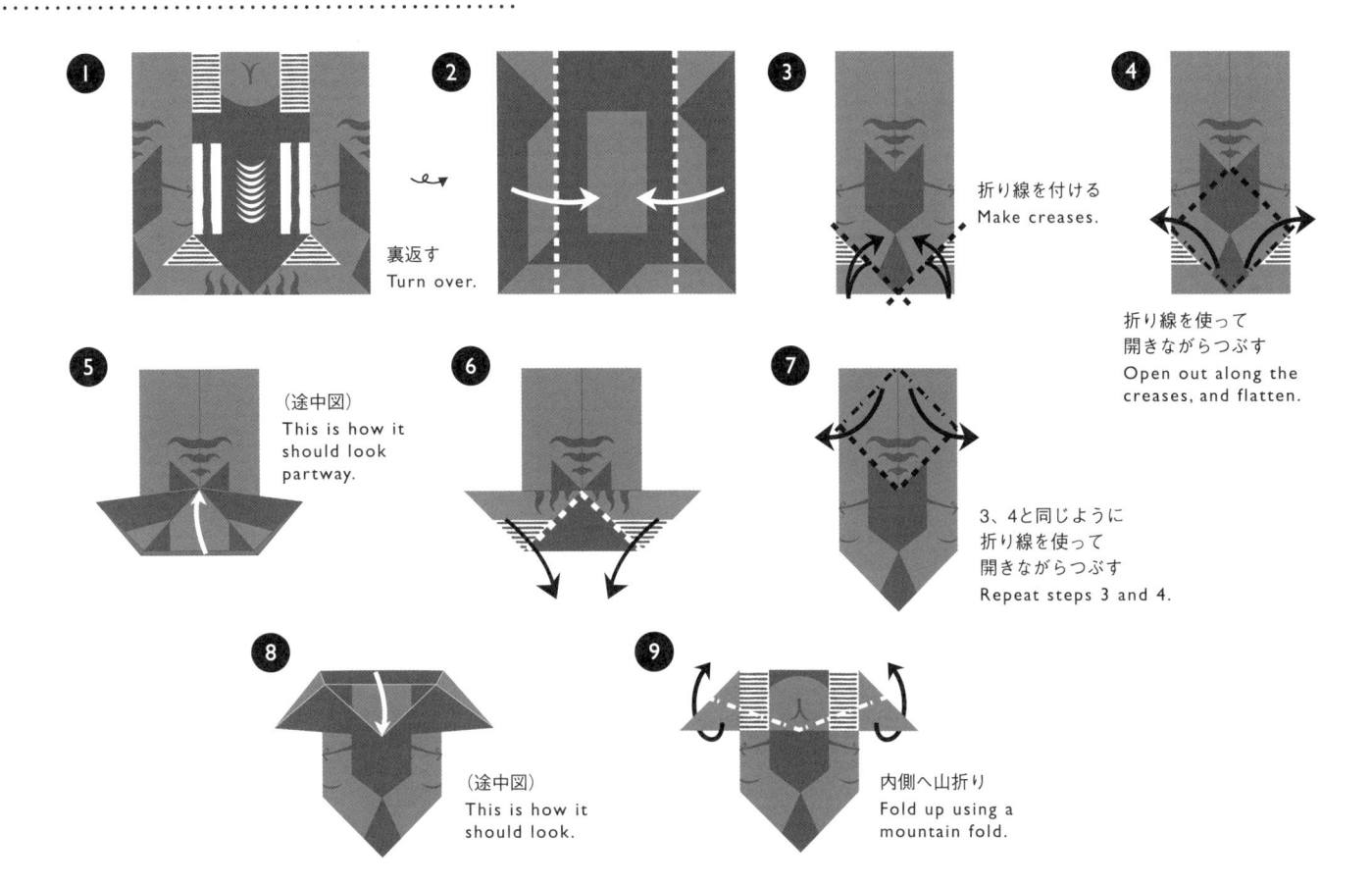

1 裏返す
Turn over.

2

3 折り線を付ける
Make creases.

4 折り線を使って開きながらつぶす
Open out along the creases, and flatten.

5 (途中図)
This is how it should look partway.

6

7 3、4と同じように折り線を使って開きながらつぶす
Repeat steps 3 and 4.

8 (途中図)
This is how it should look.

9 内側へ山折り
Fold up using a mountain fold.

⑩ ⑪ 裏返す / Turn over. ⑫ ⑬

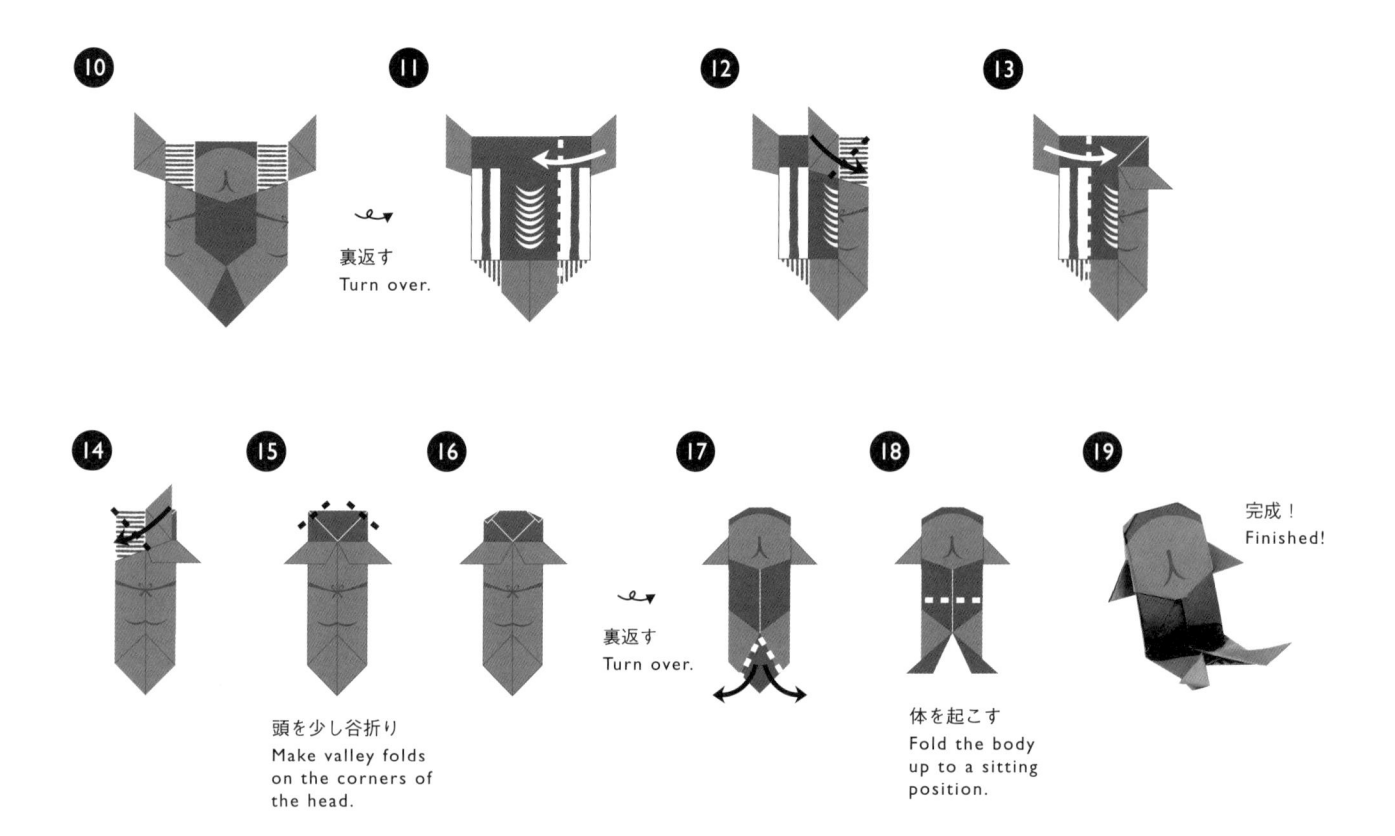

⑭ ⑮ 頭を少し谷折り / Make valley folds on the corners of the head. ⑯ 裏返す / Turn over. ⑰ ⑱ 体を起こす / Fold the body up to a sitting position. ⑲ 完成！/ Finished!

94

福助 Fukusuke → 折り紙 p63

① ② 裏返す Turn over.

③ 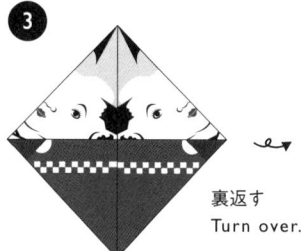 裏返す Turn over.

④ 裏側の顔を表に出すようにしながら谷折り
Make valley folds to bring the face up from behind.

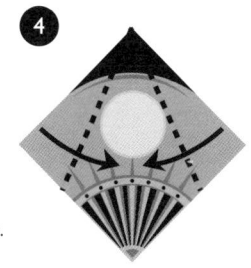

⑤ ⑥ 裏返す Turn over.

⑦ 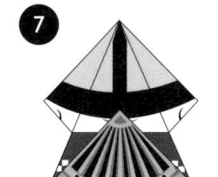 裏返す Turn over.

⑧ 頭の先を山折り
Make a mountain fold on the top of the head.

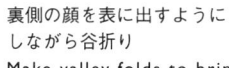

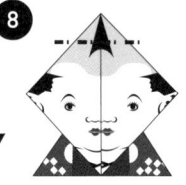

⑨ 襟元を差し込む
Tuck in the collar of his kimono.

⑩ 完成！Finished!

cochae（こちゃえ）

軸原ヨウスケと武田美貴を中心にした紙遊びのグラフィック・ユニット。「紙遊びをPOPに！」をテーマに、グラフィック折り紙、紙のパズル、新しい視点をもった玩具の製作等、幅広い活動を行っている。著書に、『妖怪おりがみ』（講談社）、『折りCA』、『百羽鶴』（青幻舎）、『ぬりえおりがみ』（ビジネス社）。2008年度グッドデザイン賞を受賞した「ファニーフェースカード」をはじめ、オリガミキットやオリガミてぬぐいなどを自主制作している。

公式ホームページ／http://www.cochae.com/

Cochae is the dynamic graphic arts unit run by Yosuke Jikuhara and Miki Takeda whose main aim is to popularize "fun with paper" through such innovative games as art origami and paper puzzles. Their publications include *Yōkai Origami*, *Ori-CA*, *Hyakuwa-zuru* and *Nurie Origami*. They have also created an origami kit and origami towel, and received a design award for their Funny Face Card.

図版協力／アド・ミュージアム東京
　　　　　愛媛県歴史文化博物館
　　　　　国立国会図書館貴重書画像データベース
　　　　　DNPアーカイブ・コム

主な参考文献／『世界大百科事典』（平凡社）
　　　　　　　『開運！招福縁起物大図鑑』（ワールドマガジン社）
　　　　　　　『京の宝づくし　縁起物』（光村推古書院）
　　　　　　　『福よ来い　古今東西めでた尽くし』（東北歴史博物館）

おとなのORIGAMI-BOOK　cochaeのグラフィック折り紙
めでた尽くし

発行日　2008年11月7日　第1刷
　　　　2025年8月18日　第9刷

著　者　cochae
発行者　篠木和久
発行所　株式会社講談社
　　　　〒112-8001 東京都文京区音羽2-12-21
　　　　電話　編集　03-5395-3560
　　　　　　　販売　03-5395-5817
　　　　　　　業務　03-5395-3615
印刷所　NISSHA株式会社
製本所　大口製本印刷株式会社

©cochae 2008, Printed in Japan

定価はカバーに表示してあります。
落丁本・乱丁本は購入書店名を明記のうえ、小社業務宛にお送り下さい。送料小社負担にてお取り替えします。なお、この本についてのお問い合わせは、第一事業本部企画部からだとこころ編集宛にお願いいたします。
本書のコピー、スキャン、デジタル化等の無断複製は著作権法上での例外を除き禁じられています。本書を代行業者等の第三者に依頼してスキャンやデジタル化することはたとえ個人や家庭内の利用でも著作権法違反です。

ISBN978-4-06-261764-2　N.D.C. 790　96p　15cm

編集協力／町田陽子、久保恵子
アートディレクション／坂川栄治
デザイン／田中久子、永井亜矢子
英訳／Ginny Tapley Takemori
英文校正／Haruko Horiuchi
撮影／講談社写真部（渡辺充俊）